COME,

Holy Spirit

Melinda Bauman

5 Fold Media
Visit us at www.5foldmedia.com

ISBN: 978-1-936578-45-0
Library of Congress Control Number: 2012946689

Endorsements

"Melinda Bauman is a lover of God and longs to see the power of God loosed in the earth today. As you read this book, you will see every side and dimension of the ministry of the Holy Spirit. Melinda shows you step-by-step the great awakenings that have taken place across America and how we should prepare for the next move of God coming on the horizon."

Dr. Jeremy Lopez
Founder of Identity Network
www.identitynetwork.net

"Melinda Bauman has written a very good book! I personally love it! She takes you on a historical journey through American times. What is revival? She clearly has the finger of God on this topic. Her explanations of understanding manifestations that may seem controversial during revival services are explained well. I recommend it to anyone who seeks what it means to be a born-again, Spirit-filled believer, learning to live in the presence of God."

Theresa Phillips
Founder of Chicago Prophetic Voice
www.chicagopropheticvoice.net

"*Come, Holy Spirit* is an overview of the work of the Holy Spirit in America from the inception of our country until today. Melinda Bauman gathers together the essential elements of God's work in our nation and calls the church to awaken to its proper place in His plan of redemption. We live in an age of sobering realities, and this book gives His people a map of the spiritual terrain their prayers need to follow for them to accompany Him safely through the dangerous events of these last days."

Joan Hunter
President, Joan Hunter Ministries
www.joanhunter.org

"In a landscape often obscured by a myriad of ideologies, theologies and doctrines, Melinda's book, *Come Holy Spirit*, is a reminder that truth is not absent and the Bible is not forgotten. Her insistence on sharing the gospel and teaching others to do so is very encouraging, especially considering that this Biblical foundation is often devalued at best. I hope this is the first of many books by Melinda Bauman that raises the bar in ministry and blazes a trail into the harvest."

Chad Taylor
www.consumingfire.com
Author, *Why Revival Still Tarries*, and *The Cry of the Harvest*

Dedication

I dedicate this book to my Lord and Savior, Jesus Christ. This book is also dedicated to you, the reader. I pray that this book will draw you closer in your walk with God. A good friend will not tell you what you want to hear, but what you need to hear. A good friend will tell you the truth, even if it may hurt. I consider you, reader, my friend. I want to share with you the full truth from the Word of God. May this book win many souls for the glory of Jesus Christ. Friend, I want to see you in heaven one day. There, everything that we have gone through on this earth will prove worthwhile. Behold, Jesus is coming very soon. May the bride of Christ be prepared, for her Bridegroom is coming.

Contents

Foreword

In her book, *Come, Holy Spirit,* Melinda Bauman will challenge you, the reader, to return to the heart of God's plan to seek and to save that which has been lost.

As a minister who has known Melinda for years as a friend, I can attest that she is a very dedicated pastor at Worldwide Great Commission Fellowship of Eastlake, Ohio, where I have ministered many times. I can also verify that she is just as serious about her region, our nation, and the world. *Come, Holy Spirit* will help bring revival back to our homes, community, and our nation—the United States of America. This book will help the church return to its roots as a nation founded upon worshipping freely, and the principles of Jesus Christ—the only hope for a hurting world.

The Lord calls us, and the Holy Spirit will confirm this in many ways. God always uses His Word as the benchmark of all truth—written and prophetic—to live and to follow our personal mandates from God. Melinda has a sincere calling to pastor a local church; yet, she also has an apostolic calling to muster the army of the Lord and herald this end time message—*Jesus IS coming again!* Melinda is called of God to invite the Holy Spirit to lead us locally, regionally, and nationally into all truth. This is a message the Lord has given her to bring to us so we would know our time is now! We must begin to cry out upon our knees, *"Come, Holy Spirit!"*

Come, Holy Spirit

Please allow Melinda's heart—bent on revival—to minister the urgency of our time for every nonbeliever to find Jesus, and for the family of God to lift Jesus higher than ever! *Come, Holy Spirit* will bring your focus back to the basics of what the Father had planned for us and for the nations to embrace the simple gospel message as Jesus demonstrated—the way, the truth, and the life.

I encourage you, the reader, to be charged with a new desire to plunge headlong into the Father's heart and not simply focus carnally upon the darkness of our nation's dilemma. Consequently, this book should shake you into a desire to become the answer, showing how we as a country were founded upon worshipping the Lord Jesus freely! Like Melinda, our hearts should be stirred to return personally and nationally to the heart of this message. *Come, Holy Spirit, we desperately need You to have Your own way in our lives and our land!*

After reading this book, please do not place it into a corner on your bookshelf, but take this message to those you personally know who need to be refueled and who in turn may invite others to renew their hearts and calling. Use this as a tool to invite friends and family into the next move of God, which our nation is now poised to experience. Just as Jesus promised, we will be a part of greater signs, wonders, and miracles as we apply the cry of *Come, Holy Spirit!*

When we are filled to overflowing with the Holy Spirit and with fire, we will burn brighter in a very dark and hurting world, ready for the beckoning call that always has shown us the way to the Father, decreeing in unison with a great declarative invitation, "Come, Holy Spirit!"

Melinda Bauman

With the same heart cry the Father has placed upon me as a voice to the nations, I highly recommend this vital tool. Use it to burn again with the mandate from the Lord to lift up Jesus. Prepare to experience all that He has brought and bought us, as we now become filled, refilled, and abundantly anointed to overflowing, continually echoing, *Come, Holy Spirit*. We so desperately need You!"

John Mark Pool
Prophetic Messenger-Author-Founder
Word to the World Ministries
www.w2wmin.org

11

Chapter 1: My Story

I received a solid foundation in faith in the Lutheran church I attended as a child. However, like many of us, I often wondered, "Is this all there is?" I sought a deeper relationship with the Lord. One day a friend invited me to attend a Pentecostal service where I encountered what my spirit had been thirsting for. I experienced the power of God in that church in a way I never had before. I was water baptized and came out of the water praising and thanking God, when suddenly I felt something touch my lips. I had been filled with the Holy Ghost and was speaking in tongues!

Almost immediately, I felt the overwhelming call into ministry. However, I did not think this strange because I believed that all Christians were called to ministry. It was some time later that I realized the magnitude of the call God had placed on my life; this was not just about ministry, but a call to preach. With this realization came fear and confusion. I had never seen a woman preach, no one told me I was called to preach, and no one helped me get into the ministry. I became so discouraged that I eventually gave up and stopped going to church.

After a period of time in this state, the Holy Spirit began to convict me. I wanted my relationship with God back. I took my focus off the call and returned it to the Savior. For many who are called into the ministry, there is a danger of putting the work of the ministry above your personal relationship with Christ; this is idolatry. We must keep our relationship with God first! Although mindful of this, I knew that God had not changed His mind about my call. As soon as I had returned to church, the call was there and I was determined to do something about it. This determination to fulfill the call marked a time of preparation. God was testing me to see if I really believed all He had spoken to me. I learned that if God speaks a thing, He will bring it to pass!

In 2000, I made up my mind to pursue my minister's license. At the same time, I began to teach Bible studies as an outreach at a local coffeehouse. In 2005, I obtained my minister's license and began to seek the Lord concerning the next step. I felt led to have monthly revival services. Despite opposition from area churches, I stepped out in faith and obedience to God. He provided a location in Wickliffe, Ohio, for the services. Signs, wonders, and miracles did follow; in each meeting, the power of God was made manifest through prophetic utterance, healing, and deliverance.

In 2007, I founded Worldwide Great Commission Fellowship. Located in Eastlake, Ohio, the church holds Sunday services and schools of ministry on weekends. I have maintained my monthly revival meetings. I continue to pursue revival in Cleveland and champion the faith through obedience to God.

To those who are called into the ministry but don't know where to start, I say, start with one-on-one ministry, which takes place on the street, on the bus, wherever you find yourself. Allow God to use you to reach out to people, and He will open doors for you. Know that God is waiting on us to take action! No one put me into the ministry—it came forth as a direct result of my relationship with the Lord. Go and do what the Bible tells you to do!

And he said unto them, Go ye into all the world, and preach the gospel to every creature (Mark 16:15).

A Word From the Lord to America, 10/5/08

I believe that the Lord is saying to America: My people, you are a nation that was founded upon righteousness and religious freedom. You are a nation with freedom of religion. Many Christians came to America to escape religious persecution in their own countries. America was the "promised land" to Christian pilgrims, a land flowing with milk and honey. My people came to America because here they were free to worship Me.

I poured out My Spirit in the 1700s at the time America was birthed as a nation. This was called the First Great Awakening. I poured out My Spirit in the 1800s when this nation was preserved and slavery ended during the Civil War. This was called the Second Great Awakening.

I poured out My Spirit in the 1900s at Azusa Street in Los Angeles, California. The Azusa Street Revival birthed the Pentecostal movement all over the world. When my people Israel became a nation in 1948, I poured out a healing revival known as the Voice of Healing. Many wonderful healings and miracles took place at this time. Then I began to pour out My Spirit upon all denominations, and this was known as the Charismatic Movement.

It is near the end of the first decade of 2000. This decade has been difficult for America. My people are wondering if I have forsaken them. In 2001, Muslim terrorists attacked

America. In 2003, America went to war with Iraq. In 2005, Hurricane Katrina destroyed New Orleans. After that, the American economy began to decline as the dollar devalued and jobs moved overseas. In 2006, the real estate market declined and houses went into foreclosure. In 2008, gas prices rose to four dollars a gallon and the stock market collapsed.

There is much worry about who the next president will be and whether or not he will bring change to America. Since 2000, my people have been wondering if I have forsaken them. America, I have not forgotten you and I have not forsaken you. We have entered into a new century, and it is time for a great outpouring of My Spirit—for a great revival.

This will be known as the Third Great Awakening. This move will be greater than any you have seen before. In this revival, My people will rise up like a mighty army and do great exploits for My glory. This revival will be known as the Saints' Movement, because the saints will rise up and operate in the power of God.

Be encouraged, My children, My people in America. You are going to be a part of the greatest revival you have ever seen. Do not give in to fear and worry because of circumstances in the world. I am in control and am preparing to usher in the Third Great Awakening. Begin to pray and seek My face. Watch what I will do. Do not be weak and faint of heart. I am looking for a strong, bold, courageous army in my church. Be strong and of good courage. Watch and see what I will do in this nation, My children, whom I love, in America.

Chapter 2: You Say You Believe, but Have You Received?

Some people wonder why there are so many different Christian denominations. In spite of all these denominations, there are many things upon which Christians agree. For instance, Christians believe in the gospel message of Jesus Christ. The word gospel means "good news," and the fact that Jesus came to seek and save that which was lost is good news indeed. Christians believe that we must be saved, or born again. We are in spiritual bondage to sin because we are sinners. In the Bible it says, "There is none righteous, no, not one." It also says, "For all have sinned, and come short of the glory of God" (Romans 3:10, 23).

Jesus died so that our sins would be forgiven and we could have eternal life. One of the best known Scriptures is John 3:16, which says, "For God so loved the world, that he gave his only begotten Son, that whosoever believeth in him should not perish, but have everlasting life."

So why does Christianity teach that we are sinners and need a Savior? Many people like to believe that they are basically good. Maybe they have lied a few times, but they have not robbed a bank or killed anybody. It takes more than doing good works or being a good person to make it to heaven. According to the Bible, we are all sinners. We are born with a fallen nature because of what happened in the garden of Eden. Adam and Eve committed the original sin by disobeying God. God commanded Adam not to eat of the tree of the knowledge of good and evil, for in that day he would die. Genesis says, "And the Lord God commanded the man, saying, Of every tree of the garden thou mayest freely eat: But of the tree of the knowledge of good and evil, thou shalt not eat of it: for in the day that thou eatest thereof thou shalt surely die" (Genesis 2:16-17).

The serpent deceived Eve, and she ate the forbidden fruit. She gave it to Adam, and he also ate it. There are two kinds of death: physical death and spiritual death. Because of sin, death entered into the world. Because we are all sinners, we will die both a physical and spiritual death. According to Romans 6:23, "For the wages of sin is death; but the gift of God is eternal life through Jesus Christ our Lord." Because God loves us, Jesus came to die on the cross so that our sins may be forgiven.

Since we are all sinners, we cannot approach a holy God. God is sinless, and He cannot be in the presence of sinful people. Our sin separates us from Him. God came to earth as Jesus Christ to die for us on the cross because He wanted this broken relationship to be restored.

So who exactly is Jesus? What do Christians believe about Jesus? Christians believe that Jesus was not just a man; He was God who came in the flesh. He was fully God and fully human at the same time. The name *Jesus* means, "Jehovah saves."[1] Jehovah God chose to manifest Himself on earth as a man, and they called His name Jesus.

---

1. Thayer and Smith, "Greek Lexicon entry for Iesous," The NAS New Testament Greek Lexicon, http://www.biblestudytools.com/lexicons/greek/nas/iesous.html (accessed April 16, 2014).

Christians believe that Jesus Christ is the only way to be saved. In John 14:6 Jesus says, "I am the way, the truth, and the life: no man cometh unto the Father, but by me." Only by receiving Jesus Christ as your Lord and Savior can you enter into the kingdom of God.

So how does a person go about receiving Jesus Christ as their Lord and Savior? We must acknowledge that we are sinners and ask Jesus to forgive us. This includes turning away from our sins, rather than continuing to live a sinful life. This is repentance.

When people repent and give their lives to Jesus, they pray the sinner's prayer. It goes something like this: *Lord Jesus, I confess that I am a sinner and need a Savior. I ask for forgiveness of my sins and ask You to be my Savior. I am trusting in You for my salvation. I believe You suffered and died on the cross and rose again from the grave to pay the full price for my sin and give me new life. I thank You for saving me. Amen.*

After a person makes a confession of faith and receives Jesus Christ as their Lord, they are baptized in water, according to Christian teachings. Baptism signifies that you are leaving the old ways behind and living a new life in Christ.

I would like to talk to you about the Comforter, the Holy Spirit. In John 14:16-17, Jesus told the disciples about the Holy Spirit. Jesus said, "And I will pray the Father, and he shall give you another Comforter, that he may abide with you for ever; even the Spirit of truth; whom the world cannot receive, because it seeth him not, neither knoweth him: but ye know him; for he dwelleth with you, and shall be in you."

Jesus later said, "These things have I spoken unto you, being yet present with you. But the Comforter, which is the

Holy Ghost, whom the Father will send in my name, he shall teach you all things, and bring all things to your remembrance, whatsoever I have said unto you" (John 14:25-26).

After Jesus was resurrected and before He ascended into heaven, He told His disciples to go to Jerusalem to wait for the promise of the Holy Spirit. After Jesus ascended into heaven, the disciples went to Jerusalem to wait for the promise of the Holy Spirit and pray in the upper room. On the day of Pentecost, the Holy Spirit was poured out. There were many people in Jerusalem at this time, and the way the disciples were acting after being filled with the Holy Spirit attracted their attention. The people made fun of the disciples and even accused them of drunkenness. Peter explained the amazing behavior in Acts 2:15-18:

> *For these are not drunken, as ye suppose, seeing it is but the third hour of the day. But this is that which was spoken by the prophet Joel; and it shall come to pass in the last days, saith God, I will pour out of my Spirit upon all flesh: and your sons and your daughters shall prophesy, and your young men shall see visions, and your old men shall dream dreams: and on my servants and on my handmaidens I will pour out in those days of my Spirit; and they shall prophesy.*

Peter preached to them about Jesus Christ, and the people became convicted. They asked Peter what they should do to get saved. That day, many people made a decision to follow Christ because they saw the change in the disciples.

I assume that those reading this book have heard the gospel message of Jesus Christ. You know that you are sinners, saved by grace. You know that Jesus died on the cross to take away your sins, and you may already have prayed the sinner's prayer and invited Jesus into your heart, perhaps you have even followed up your decision with water baptism.

You say that you believe, but I wonder, have you received everything that God has for you? Have you received the baptism of the Holy Spirit, as the disciples did when they spoke in tongues? Have you had your Pentecostal experience? Have you been filled with the Holy Ghost the way the disciples were in the upper room?

It is not difficult to receive the baptism of the Holy Ghost. Simply believe and ask God.

Chapter 3: First and Second Great Awakenings in America

In the church world, people talk about the need for revival. Churches hold prayer meetings and pray for revival. What is a religious revival? It is a spiritual awakening in which people turn to God and the Holy Spirit is poured out. In the Bible, the Holy Spirit was first poured out on the day of Pentecost. When the believers received the power of the Holy Spirit, they were able to spread the gospel and do the works of ministry. Miracles and healing were common in the early church. Acts 5:12 says, "And by the hands of the apostles were many signs and wonders wrought among the people." Verse 16 says, "There came also a multitude out of the cities round about unto Jerusalem, bringing sick folks, and them which were vexed with unclean spirits: and they were healed every one."

At various times in history, the Lord has breathed new life into the church and brought in multitudes of new believers. Widespread repentance and enthusiasm about the things of God characterize such seasons of blessing. Revival happens when God pours out His Spirit on all flesh.

It is the goal of every Christian to spread the gospel message of salvation through Jesus Christ. During revival, many people come to the Lord and commit their lives to Him. In the times we are living in, people are troubled and are looking for answers. There seems to be instability, moral decline, and much uncertainty on earth today. Where do we turn? Who has the answers for the world's problems? Perhaps we should read 2 Chronicles 7:14: "If my people, which are called by my name, shall humble themselves, and pray, and seek my face, and turn from their wicked ways; then will I hear from heaven, and will forgive their sin, and will heal their land." God wants people to pray and cry out to Him for revival.

Throughout church history, there have been dark periods as well as times of revival. Two significant revivals have impacted American history. These revivals are called the First and Second Great Awakenings. The First Great Awakening occurred between 1727 and 1745 and swept through the American colonies. It changed the political and social thought of the colonists and set the stage for the American Revolution against Britain. It is important to understand the religious situation that drew Americans into resistance with Britain.

In the 1730s, ministers began to travel throughout the colonies and preach about God. These evangelists were lay ministers, and they would present a message of salvation that would move and inspire their audience. The preachers at times became frenzied, and the congregation often wept aloud and screamed. These evangelists appealed so greatly to the public that they drew huge crowds. The result was that a religious revival, intended to preach salvation, gave rise to political and social unrest that challenged traditional societal roles. The revival had lasting social effects as a more tolerant and democratic spirit began to emerge in the colonies. The common man had a feeling of self-worth, and people assumed new responsibilities in religious affairs. These attitudes were the beginnings of a sense of independence and equality that later set the stage for the American Revolution. The spirit of independence was proclaimed in the colonies by the

Declaration of Independence, which the local clergy often rose to read to their congregations. This spirit helped spark independence in America.

The Second Great Awakening occurred between 1790 and 1830. One impact of this revival was the abolitionist movement against slavery. Some northern churches denounced slavery as sin and called for immediate abolition. The Civil War convinced Northerners that God's will was not only the preservation of the Union, but also the demise of slavery. During the Civil War, President Lincoln announced his intention to free the slaves in the south. Without the church's support, it is unlikely that the president could have proceeded as he did. On at least three occasions, Lincoln proclaimed public fast days: he urged Americans to go to their houses of worship, confess their sins humbly to God, and ask God's blessing. These times of confession provided opportunities for ministers to express their conviction that the war was necessary to achieve God's appointed purpose—a preserved Union.

The nineteenth century birthed many different Christian denominations in America. But by the 1830s, almost all of these bodies had a deep evangelical emphasis in common. The core experience of this evangelicalism was conversion. Christianity was not simply something that people believed, but something that happened to them, involving a real, intensely emotional conversion event. They experienced a profound transformation, which left them with a changed sense of self, and an identity as a Christian.

A distinguishing feature of this evangelicalism was its approach to religious revivals. The phrase "religious revival" was coined to describe a new phenomenon in which churches experienced an unexpected awakening of spiritual concern. There was a special outpouring of God's saving grace, which led to unprecedented numbers of intense and surprising conversions that revived the piety and power of the churches.

These revivals first emerged at the turn of the nineteenth century, with the invention of the camp meeting in western Virginia, North Carolina, and on the Kentucky and Ohio frontier. At these meetings—the most famous of which took place at Cane Ridge, Kentucky in 1801—hundreds, sometimes thousands, of people would gather from miles around in a wilderness encampment. There they engaged in a series of meetings designed to promote religious fervor and conversion. These meetings included the singing of hymns, public confessions, turning from sin, and collective prayer. Powerful and well-known preachers delivered sermons.

At these meetings, people were convinced that they were experiencing a visitation of the Holy Spirit such as the early church had known at Pentecost. When a wave of emotional conversions occurred, the people believed it was of God. At the Cane Ridge Revival, people were deeply affected, and strong emotional responses were considered proof of conversion. Sometimes people fainted and fell to the ground. There was dancing, running, and singing—all of which were manifestations of God's presence. The noise of the meeting was so great that some said the noise was like the roar of Niagara Falls. Meetings continued all day, often going late into the night. People prayed fervently and worshipped God with great joy. The impact of the Holy Spirit produced new levels of unity, joy, and changed lives.

The evangelical revival produced movements, including the holiness churches of the nineteenth century. Those movements prepared the way for the development of the Pentecostal churches and, later, the Charismatic Movement of the twentieth century.

Melinda Bauman

In 1901, a man name Charles Parham conducted classes at a Bible college in Kansas. When Parham laid hands on a woman in his class and prayed for her to be baptized in the Holy Spirit, she began to speak in tongues. Soon Parham and the students also spoke in tongues. They taught that the gift of tongues was the initial evidence of the baptism in the Holy Spirit.

Chapter 4: The Azusa Street Revival and Pentecost

Los Angeles, California, was a popular destination at the turn of the twentieth century for Americans who dreamed of greater opportunities and purpose. By 1906, this city was a major hub of activity. In April of that year, two events focused the world's attention on Los Angeles: the city was impacted by an earthquake that also devastated San Francisco, and services conducted in a small holiness mission on Azusa Street birthed global spiritual renewal. Thousands of individuals converged on the city to attend the revival at Azusa Street's mission, where they found a renewed purpose and passion in serving Jesus Christ, and were commissioned to share the message of His love and power with others. Almost a century later, the activities of the renowned Azusa Street outpouring in Los Angeles are still hailed as one of the greatest events in Christian history. Today, Pentecostal and charismatic believers throughout the world point to the significance of Azusa Street in their spiritual heritage and development.

Los Angeles was not the only place where this spiritual renewal was being made manifest. The Spirit of God was being poured out in other parts of the world simultaneously. Revival was sweeping parts of Europe, specifically Wales. Among the spiritual manifestations accompanying these outpourings were remarkable healings, complete transformations of

29

lifestyle, deliverance from ungodly habits, and utterances in languages unknown to the speaker. Since the days of the early apostles in the Bible, there are recordings throughout history of people speaking in languages unknown to them.

To those who met at Azusa Street, the revival was viewed as a sign of the restoration of New Testament Christianity. These early Pentecostals believed they were experiencing the same infilling of God's power that the apostles had on the day of Pentecost. Obeying the commands of Jesus upon His ascension, the early apostles had gathered together in Jerusalem to await the promised Holy Spirit who empowered the Christian church to complete the work Christ had started on earth. Christians in Los Angeles had been praying for revival and seeking more of God for several years prior to the 1906 outpouring. Consumed with the desire for more of God, these people prayed, witnessed, preached, and prophesied about an outpouring of God's Spirit.

Meanwhile, William Seymour was traveling throughout the United States in search of a better life. An African American from Louisiana, he was the son of former slaves. He became a preacher following a severe case of smallpox that left him blind in one eye and facially disfigured. In 1905, Seymour traveled to Houston, Texas. Charles Parham, the Bible professor from Kansas, was in Houston conducting classes on the topic of the Holy Spirit. Seymour attended Parham's meetings. Although Seymour had not yet received the baptism of the Holy Spirit evidenced by speaking in other tongues, he preached that message with great fervency. Seymour traveled to Los Angeles, California, in February 1906 and began preaching at a holiness church. Some in the congregation were hungering for more of God and felt compelled to spend hours in prayer.

30

Several experienced visions that God was about to bless Los Angeles with a spiritual outpouring.

The group continued to gather for prayer and worship, conducting services in a home at Bonnie Brae Street. Others began to attend the meetings, including some white families from nearby holiness churches. On April 9, 1906, a breakthrough occurred when a man, who had been praying with Seymour, was baptized with the Holy Spirit and began to speak in other tongues. The Spirit of God moved, and six others began to speak in tongues that same evening. A woman began to sing in tongues and play the piano under the power of God. On April 12, Seymour received the baptism of the Holy Spirit after praying all night.

Following the initial outpouring of the Holy Spirit in Los Angeles, interest grew in the prayer meetings. The crowds became too large for the home. The group discovered an available building at 312 Azusa Street. Within days, the media learned of the revival services conducted at the Azusa Street Mission, and newspaper reports were published throughout the United States and the world. Thousands learned of the revival and were drawn to the meetings. They all came together in worship: men, women, children, black, white, Hispanic, Asian, rich, poor, illiterate, and educated. They flocked to Los Angeles with both skepticism and spiritual hunger.

In September 1906, a local newspaper wrote this about the Azusa Street meetings: "They cry and make noises all day and into the night. They run, jump, shake all over, shout at the top of their lungs, spin around in circles, and fall onto the floor jerking, kicking, and rolling. Some of them pass out and do not move for hours as though they were dead. These people claim to be filled with the Holy Spirit. They have a black man as their preacher who stays on his knees most of the time. They repeatedly sing the same song, the Comforter has come."[2]

The river of God's Spirit was flowing mightily in Los Angeles. God was faithful in answering prayer, for revival had come. Within months, the Azusa Street Mission had as many as 1,300 attending their services, making them the largest congregation in the city. The revival fervor continued for three years. Services were held three times daily, often without a break. The message was the love of God, and that unity and equality were priorities. Racism was washed away. Women were provided positions of leadership. A newsletter reported, "One token of the Lord's coming is that He is melting all races and nations together, and they are filled with the power and glory of God. He is baptizing by one Spirit into one body and making up a people that will be ready to meet Him when He comes."[3]

As a direct result of the Azusa Street outpouring, thousands of people were led into a deeper relationship with Jesus Christ. People began to study the Word of God, become convicted of sin, and surrender their lives to Jesus Christ. They were baptized with the Holy Ghost who led and guided them into greater spiritual truths found in the Bible. The Spirit of God empowered them with boldness to fulfill the Great Commission. Signs and wonders followed those who believed: the blind saw, the deaf heard, the mute spoke, the lame walked, and the dead were raised to life. Such reports are commonplace among the early Pentecostal believers, and all of these signs testify of the glory and power of Jesus Christ. These Spirit-filled believers considered themselves to

2. Larry Martin, *The Life and Ministry of William J. Seymour; and a History of the Azusa Street Revival*, (Christian Life Books: Joplin, MO), 248-249.
3. Ibid, 197.

be witnesses, and many sailed to foreign lands as missionaries
to share the gospel message.

This movement of God was not only for Los Angeles, but
the whole world—even future generations. What happened at
Azusa Street helped renew Christianity, bringing fresh vision
and passion to the Great Commission. Consumed with zeal for
God and empowered by the Holy Spirit, people took the Word
of God all over the world. As a result, many have learned of
the love and grace of God. The same power of God is still
filling people with the Holy Spirit and leading them to spread
the gospel around the world. Today there are more than 600
million Pentecostal and charismatic believers.

In 1910, William Seymour prophesied that in one
hundred years there would be an outpouring of God's Spirit
and His Shekinah glory that would be greater and more far-
reaching than what was experienced at Azusa. As people
begin to believe that God will again pour out His Spirit as
was prophesied during the Azusa Revival, hope is being
restored and expectations are rising.

May we continue to go forward in the power of the
Holy Spirit as witnesses and ministers to reach the world
for Jesus Christ.

Chapter 5: Speaking in Tongues

Following water baptism, one should pray to be filled with the Holy Spirit, as evidenced by speaking in tongues. In the Christian world, there has been much confusion and misunderstanding concerning speaking in tongues. What does the Bible say about tongues?

After Jesus resurrected from the dead, He appeared to His disciples many times. When He ascended into heaven, He gave them instructions to go into Jerusalem and wait for the promise of the Holy Spirit.

On the day of Pentecost, the Holy Spirit was poured out in the upper room in Jerusalem. The people who heard the disciples speaking in tongues were confused and even accused them of being drunk. Peter stood up and began to explain what was going on. In Acts chapter 10, Peter was sent to the house of Cornelius, a Gentile, to share the gospel message. While he was speaking to them, the Holy Ghost came and filled them too, and they began to speak with other tongues, which was evidence that they had been filled with the Spirit.

During His ministry, Jesus referred to the Holy Spirit as living water. John 7:37-39 says,

> *In the last day, that great day of the feast, Jesus stood and cried, saying, If any man thirst, let him come unto me, and drink. He that believeth on me, as the scripture hath said, out of his belly shall*

*flow rivers of living water. (But this spake he of
the Spirit, which they that believe on him should
receive: for the Holy Ghost was not yet given;
because that Jesus was not yet glorified.)*

Jesus said one of the signs that would follow believers is
tongues. Mark 16:17 says, "And these signs shall follow them
that believe; in my name shall they cast out devils; they shall
speak with new tongues."

Jesus assures us that if we ask for the Holy Spirit, He
will give it to us. Baptism of the Holy Spirit means that we
have the very presence of God inside us. It transforms us and
gives us power to live a righteous life. Many people today
seem to be afraid. They are searching for a sense of security.
Many people feel an emptiness inside which they try to fill
with different things. We seek fulfillment and meaning in life.
This emptiness can only be satisfied by a relationship with
Jesus Christ. When the Holy Spirit comes into our lives, He
brings joy, peace, and love.

The Holy Spirit is the power that raised Jesus from the
dead. Romans 8:11 says, "But if the Spirit of him that raised
up Jesus from the dead dwell in you, he that raised up Christ
from the dead shall also quicken your mortal bodies by his
Spirit that dwelleth in you."

When John the Baptist baptized Jesus in the Jordan River,
the Holy Spirit descended upon Him like a dove. Jesus did
His supernatural works through the power of the Holy Spirit.
He performed miracles, healed the sick, raised the dead, and
cast out devils. If we have the same Holy Spirit that Jesus
had, we are also able to do the works that Jesus did. In John
14:12-13 Jesus says, "Verily, verily, I say unto you, He that
believeth on me, the works that I do shall he do also; and

greater works than these shall he do; because I go unto my Father. And whatsoever ye shall ask in my name, that will I do, that the Father may be glorified in the Son."

When we are filled with the Holy Spirit, we receive the potential to operate in the power of God. Jesus gave us the authority to do the works of the ministry, to witness to others, and to reach the lost. The Holy Spirit gives us boldness to spread the gospel. The disciples prayed for boldness in Acts 4:29-31,

> *And now, Lord, behold their threatenings: and grant unto thy servants, that with all boldness they may speak thy word, by stretching forth thine hand to heal; and that signs and wonders may be done by the name of thy holy child Jesus. And when they had prayed, the place was shaken where they were assembled together; and they were all filled with the Holy Ghost, and they spake the word of God with boldness.*

The Holy Spirit helps us to pray. When we pray in tongues, the Holy Spirit prays through us. Romans 8:26-27 says, "Likewise the Spirit also helpeth our infirmities: for we know not what we should pray for as we ought: but the Spirit itself maketh intercession for us with groanings which cannot be uttered. And he that searcheth the hearts knoweth what is the mind of the Spirit, because he maketh intercession for the saints according to the will of God."

The Holy Spirit teaches and guides us. Jesus says, "These things have I spoken unto you, being yet present with you. But the Comforter, which is the Holy Ghost, whom the Father will send in my name, he shall teach you all things, and bring all things to your remembrance, whatsoever I have said unto you" (John 14:25-26). In John 16:13 Jesus says, "Howbeit when he, the Spirit of truth, is come, he will guide you into all truth: for he shall not speak of himself; but whatsoever he shall hear, that shall he speak: and he will shew you things to come."

God wants us to be filled with the Holy Spirit and led by the Spirit. Romans 8:14-16 says, "For as many as are led by the Spirit of God, they are the sons of God. For ye have not received the spirit of bondage again to fear; but ye have received the Spirit of adoption, whereby we cry, Abba, Father. The Spirit itself beareth witness with our spirit, that we are the children of God."

The baptism of the Holy Spirit opens the door to the gifts of the Spirit. Having the Holy Spirit makes you eligible to receive spiritual gifts. It is like the entryway to the supernatural realm of God.

The baptism of the Holy Spirit, evidenced by speaking in tongues, is for all people who believe. The supernatural power of God that we read about in the Bible is for today. God is able to use you just like He used the disciples.

Chapter 6: How to Receive the Baptism of the Holy Spirit

Tongues are the sign, or evidence, of the Holy Spirit. When a person receives the baptism of the Holy Spirit evidenced by speaking in tongues, this is part of the process of becoming born again. Being born again does not refer to a physical rebirth, but a spiritual one. When we become born again and are saved, we are like spiritual babies. Jesus said that we cannot enter the kingdom of heaven unless we become as little children. Matthew 19:13-14 says, "Then were there brought unto him little children, that he should put his hands on them, and pray: and the disciples rebuked them. But Jesus said, Suffer little children, and forbid them not, to come unto me: for of such is the kingdom of heaven."

How does a little child behave? Children have a very simple faith. They look up to their parents and just believe. They do not question, but simply reach out in faith.

Jesus said we must be like children in order to receive from the Lord. We must have an attitude of total trust in God. Parents know that teaching obedience to their children is a major challenge. Obedience is based on trust, and we hope that our children will trust us and believe that we know what is best for them. Many people have a hard time trusting or believing in God. It is God's will that we read the Bible, believe what it says, and obey it.

Becoming born again is the new birth experience. Little babies depend totally on their parents, and God wants us to depend on Him. We are like children before our heavenly Father. When we are saved, we get a new father. God becomes our Father, and we become His children. We are adopted into the family of God (see Galatians 4:4-6).

Receiving the Holy Spirit is part of the new birth process. When a baby is born and takes its first breath, it begins to cry. This is how we know the baby is alive. Speaking in tongues is the evidence that someone has received the Holy Spirit.

Why did God choose tongues as the sign of Holy Spirit baptism? Talking is our chief means of communication, and the Holy Spirit is expressed through our voice. The tongue is one of the hardest things to control, and yet is the very thing that can bring life or death to us. Many of us have said things that we shouldn't have said, and our words may have gotten us into a lot of trouble. It is hard to take words back once we have said them. Our words can cause much good, but also much hurt. That is why we should choose carefully what comes out of our mouths. Parents especially should be sure to speak positive and encouraging words over their children.

Perhaps it is a good thing that God chose to get control of our tongue through the Holy Spirit. When we speak in tongues, we yield our speech to Him.

So now we come to the place where we can pray for the Holy Spirit baptism. When you pray, be comfortable. You can be sitting or kneeling. People receive the Holy Spirit in different places. You may be in bed at night, you may be in your kitchen cooking, or you may be driving your car. Some receive the baptism of the Holy Spirit in church when other people are praying with them, and some receive it when they are at home alone. It doesn't matter where you are or whom you are with—the important thing is that you receive it!

Ask and believe for God's gift. You must believe that God has a very special gift for you, and He wants you to have this gift. True faith always is demonstrated by obedience. Hebrews 11:6 says, "But without faith it is impossible to please him: for he that cometh to God must believe that he is, and that he is a rewarder of them that diligently seek him." Those who ask and believe can be assured of receiving the Holy Spirit. As a loving parent would hand out a gift to His child, Jesus is offering you the Holy Spirit. All you have to do is receive Him.

Begin your prayer by praising and worshipping God. Nothing pleases God more than our worship and praise. What better way can we demonstrate our faith in His promises than by thanking and worshipping Him before the gift is given? Hebrews 13:15 says, "By him therefore let us offer the sacrifice of praise to God continually, that is, the fruit of our lips giving thanks to his name." Psalm 95:2 says, "Let us come before his presence with thanksgiving, and make a joyful noise unto him with psalms."

Pray to God from your heart. Say something like this:

Dear Jesus, I want to thank You for the baptism of the Holy Spirit. You already have shown me love by forgiving my sins and cleansing me with Your blood. I believe that the Holy Spirit will fill me with power, love, peace, and joy. Your Word says that You want me to have the Holy Spirit. So here I am in Your presence like a child, asking and believing that rivers of living water will begin to flow out of my innermost being.

41

Come, Holy Spirit

This is just a sample prayer. Talk to God in your own words, like you are having a conversation with a good friend. An expression of gratitude and faith always merits a divine response. In order to receive the Holy Spirit, your mouth must be open. When I received Him, I was thanking and praising God. I was looking up and my hands were raised. Next thing I knew, I saw a bright white light. Then a feeling of power came down upon me. I felt a tingling, or heaviness, on my tongue. As I continued to worship God, the preacher told me I was speaking in tongues.

We do not try to learn how to speak in tongues. We are seeking the Holy Spirit. When the Spirit comes inside, He will take over your language. Let the Spirit submerge and flow out of you. If you feel something on your tongue, just yield to that. The Holy Spirit is coming in. With the Holy Spirit living inside you, you will speak in tongues. At the same time, you will probably feel great peace, joy, and love.

Many people have difficulty receiving the Holy Spirit because they think they have to understand the process first. Just yield to God and receive. Once you receive the Spirit, you will be led to all knowledge and truth. The Holy Spirit will speak to you, teaching and guiding you. Once you are filled with the Spirit, you will be able to understand the Bible better.

Some people are afraid of the supernatural, unknown qualities of the Holy Spirit. You don't need to be afraid because the Bible says the Holy Spirit is God. If this is true, then you should want to have Him within you. The Holy Spirit will greatly change your life for the better. You will feel a happiness that you have never known before. This happiness comes from God, not from the world.

In order to receive the Spirit, we must surrender to His control. This is difficult for many people to do, but you must trust God enough to give Him total control of your life. When you surrender your control and yield to God, the Holy Spirit will come in. When you first begin to receive the Spirit, you may sound like you are babbling. But eventually this will develop into words of a language you have never learned. This is similar to a baby learning to talk. At first the baby babbles, then it begins to speak real words. As spiritually newborn babies, this same process can occur within us. When the Spirit begins to come in, you may have stammering lips. If this happens, just continue to pray and yield and you will begin speaking in tongues. The Spirit will not force you to speak in tongues, but if you submit yourself, the Spirit will come in. When you become filled, welcome to a brand new life! Are you ready to pray for the baptism of the Holy Spirit?

Chapter 7: Welcome Holy Spirit Wind and Fire

After Jesus was resurrected from the dead, He appeared to His disciples many times. When He ascended into heaven, He gave them instructions to go into Jerusalem and wait for the promise of the Holy Spirit. On the day of Pentecost, the Holy Spirit was poured out in the upper room in Jerusalem. Besides the wind and tongues of fire, another sign was observed: when believers received the Holy Spirit, speaking in tongues was the sign that they had been filled. The disciples received the Holy Spirit and spoke in tongues on the day of Pentecost.

On the day of Pentecost, the Holy Spirit blew into the room like a mighty rushing wind. John 3:8 says, "The wind bloweth where it listeth, and thou hearest the sound thereof, but canst not tell whence it cometh, and whither it goeth: so is every one that is born of the Spirit."

Wind is a force that we cannot see, but we can see its effects. We see the leaves moving on a tree or a can rolling down the street. On a windy day, you have to hold onto your hat so it won't fly off your head. I was at a church service once where the praise and worship was very intense. People were genuinely worshipping God with their whole heart. I was at the back of the church, and I looked toward the front. I didn't see anything exactly, but what seemed like a wind fell upon the people all at once. The people began moving around like leaves blowing in the wind. Then the glory of God came and took over the service. I call this a Holy Ghost takeover, or a visitation. When this happened, God began to move and minister to the people.

I was raised in a non-Spirit-filled Protestant church. As I got older, I began a deeper search for God. When I was twenty, a friend invited me to her Pentecostal church. When I walked into the doors of that church, I knew something was different. I could sense something in the air, and I observed the people. The service had not yet started, and people were in prayer. They were on their knees at the altar in front of the church. Some were sitting in their seats. Most of them were praying out loud, spontaneously, and from their hearts. This was a new experience for me.

My childhood church used mostly formal prayers that the congregation would repeat after the pastor. The people in this Pentecostal church were praying out loud, some in English and some in unknown tongues. I had never encountered this before, and I asked my friend what was going on. I asked her what it was that I felt in that sanctuary. She explained to me that I was experiencing the presence of the Holy Spirit. She said the Holy Spirit is the presence of God, which you can feel in the air around you.

As the people intensified their prayers, the presence of the Holy Spirit increased in the church. I was told that the Holy Spirit can exist or move in the air, as well as dwell inside a person. This is known as the baptism of the Holy Spirit; when a person is filled, they will speak in other tongues. This experienced is outlined in the description of the day of Pentecost in Acts 2:1-4.

46

I found all this information quite interesting and amazing as I listened to the people around me pray in tongues. The worship service started, and I gained more new experiences. I observed people worshipping freely and openly. I had never seen that in church before. They were standing up, their hands raised, and singing out loud. Some were crying, others were speaking in tongues, shaking, laughing, clapping, or jumping. I even saw a couple of the men take off running around the church!

Some went to the front for prayer, and when the pastor laid hands on them, they fell down! I later learned they were being slain in the Spirit. All of this was going on before the pastor had even preached the sermon! I suppose some people may think, "Those church people are acting crazy. Let's get out of here fast!" But I did not think that way. As a matter of fact, I was enthralled, captivated, and fascinated!

You see, God knew what I needed. When I saw those Spirit-filled people, I realized that they knew something I didn't and had something I didn't. I did not totally understand the baptism of the Holy Spirit at that time, but I made it my business to learn. In 1990, in that Pentecostal church, God filled me with the wonderful baptism of His Holy Spirit, which changed my life forever.

On the day of Pentecost, the Holy Spirit appeared to the disciples as flames of fire. Hebrews 12:29 says, "For our God is a consuming fire." In 1990, God filled me with the Holy Ghost and fire. At that time, I got my marching orders: To go be a fire starter. God has put a fire in me that cannot be quenched. It is like fire shut up in my bones. I cannot keep silent about it! If you woke up in the middle of the night and your house was on fire, would you roll over and go back to sleep? No! You would jump up, call 9-1-1, and yell, "Fire!

Fire! Fire!" When we are filled with the baptism of the Holy Ghost evidenced by speaking in tongues, we are set on fire!

When Elijah prepared his altar in the Old Testament, fire fell from heaven and consumed the altar. Has your altar been consumed by fire from heaven? Have you been roasted, toasted, and consumed with the fire of God? I was talking with someone about revival in Cleveland, Ohio, and they asked, "In which church is the revival going to break out?" In the 1990s, the Toronto Revival and the Brownsville Revival occurred. God has shown me here in Cleveland that brushfires are breaking out in different area churches. As the brushfires burn, they will join together in unity to produce an unstoppable and great wildfire—a Holy Ghost inferno! So the answer to the question is: it's going to break out in all churches that want revival! Let revival fire fall!

In August 2009, we were holding a revival service. Worship started at 7 p.m. and around 7:30, someone came to tell me an alarm was going off in the church building. I went to investigate, and sure enough an alarm was ringing. Three policemen arrived a few minutes later, and I apologized to them because there was no sign of fire or explanation for the alarm. The sermon that night was about revival fire, and the fire of the Holy Spirit falling in Ohio was our decree. After the service, a woman told me that she had a testimony. When she was driving in her car earlier that day, she smelled smoke and fire. The smell lasted until she arrived home. Another woman said that when she was at home earlier that day, she smelled smoke and thought that something was burning in her house.

When we went to the parking lot after the service, people said that the electricity had gone out in different parts of the city around the church. They said an electric transformer had caught fire and thousands of people had lost power. Someone told me that a friend had to borrow her generator because the electricity had gone out at her house. I began to put the pieces of the puzzle together and realized that God was releasing signs of revival fire!

Before Jesus began His ministry, a man was sent to prepare the way of the Lord. The name of this messenger was John the Baptist. John was the forerunner sent to awaken the Jewish people and prepare them for the coming of Jesus Christ the Messiah. John the Baptist preached a message of repentance, and he baptized people in the Jordan River. Some of the people who came to be baptized by John thought that he was the Messiah. John told them that he was not the Messiah, but that there was one to come who would be mightier than him.

John the Baptist baptized Jesus. John recognized Jesus as the Messiah. John did not feel worthy to baptize Jesus and tried to refuse. Jesus told him that it was necessary to fulfill all righteousness. John had said that the Messiah who was to come would baptize with more than water. John says in Matthew 3:11, "I indeed baptize you with water unto repentance: but he that cometh after me is mightier than I, whose shoes I am not worthy to bear: he shall baptize you with the Holy Ghost, and with fire."

Jesus is the baptizer with the Holy Ghost and fire! Have you received the baptism of the Holy Spirit like the disciples did when they spoke in tongues? Have you had your Pentecostal experience? Have you been filled with the Holy Ghost the way they were filled in the upper room? Receive the fire of the Holy Ghost!

Chapter 8: Holy Ghost Power

Jesus Christ came to bring salvation to the world through His death, burial, and resurrection. While He was on earth, Jesus preached the gospel, healed the sick, cast out demons, and performed miracles. Jesus was filled with the power of the Holy Spirit when John the Baptist baptized Him. After John the Baptist was thrown into prison, he sent men to ask Jesus if He was the Messiah, wondering if they should look for another. Jesus wanted John to know that He was truly the Messiah, so he pointed him to the signs that were happening. Everywhere Jesus went He performed signs, wonders, and miracles. Jesus operated in the power of the Holy Spirit when He cast demons out of a man. Luke 4:33-36 says,

And in the synagogue there was a man, which had a spirit of an unclean devil, and cried out with a loud voice, saying, Let us alone; what have we to do with thee, thou Jesus of Nazareth? art thou come to destroy us? I know thee who thou art; the Holy One of God. And Jesus rebuked him, saying, Hold thy peace, and come out of him. And when the devil had thrown him in the midst, he came out of him, and hurt him not. And they were all amazed, and spake among themselves, saying, What a word is this! for with authority and power he commandeth the unclean spirits, and they come out.

Jesus operated in the power of the Holy Spirit when He healed the sick. The religious leaders were very skeptical of Jesus, and they did not believe that He was the Son of God. Jesus told them to believe in Him because of the works that He did. In John 10:37-38 Jesus said, "If I do not the works of my Father, believe me not. But if I do, though ye believe not me, believe the works: that ye may know, and believe, that the Father is in me, and I in him."

Before Jesus ascended into heaven, He told His followers to go wait in Jerusalem for the promise of the Holy Spirit. The disciples waited in the upper room until the Holy Spirit was poured out on the day of Pentecost. When the day came, they were filled with the power of the Holy Spirit which was evidenced by speaking in tongues. The Greek word for "power" in the Bible is *dunamis*. The definition of *dunamis* is "power for performing miracles."[4] *Dunamis* is similar to the word dynamite. When dynamite goes off, there is explosive power. Jesus operated in dunamis power. The disciples also operated in this dunamis power when they performed miracles. When we are filled with the Holy Ghost, we receive the dunamis power to perform supernatural works. Through the power of the Holy Ghost, we can perform signs, wonders, and miracles.

In August 2003, I was working at my computer. The computer flickered briefly, and I thought, *That was strange.* Things seemed to be okay for another minute, but then the lights and computers went out for good. People were making phone calls, and trying to figure out what was going on. My coworkers told me there was a major power outage which had

4. Thayer and Smith. "Greek Lexicon entry for Dunamis," The NAS New Testament Greek Lexicon, http://www.biblestudytools.com/lexicons/greek/nas/dunamis.html (accessed April 16, 2014).

affected the whole of eastern United States. I decided that the best thing to do was head home. There was gridlock because the traffic lights were not working. While I endured the drive home, I scanned the radio stations. Only one station was broadcasting. I knew it was useless to go to the bank, store, or gas station because cash registers would not be working.

When I got home, there were no lights, no air conditioning, no refrigerator, no stove, no computer, and no radio. It was an eerie feeling. I turned on my battery-powered shortwave radio and got out candles for when it got dark. The phone worked, so I called a couple of people to tell them I was okay. Sometime during the night, the electricity came back on. Eventually things went back to normal, but people were shaken up and forced to realize how much they depend on power.

Without electricity, we cannot cook, keep anything cold, buy anything at the store, or get money from the bank. If the power had been out for many days, life would have become very difficult, even miserable. What would the church be like if it had no power? Life would be miserable. The church needs spiritual power which is the power of the Holy Spirit. Unfortunately, much of the church world is suffering today because they have no spiritual power. They are not preaching the baptism of the Holy Ghost as described in Acts 2, and people are not filled with power from on high. If the church is not filled with the Holy Ghost, they are in a power blackout.

When there is a power blackout, we cannot function properly. When the church is in a spiritual blackout, there is no power. There are no miracles or healings. There are no signs and wonders. The church is basically dead. There is no anointing, because the Holy Spirit is not there. If the electricity went out at your house, you would notice it right away. The sad thing is that most of these churches don't even know they are in a blackout. They don't know what they are missing. We must be filled with the dunamis power of the Holy Spirit!

The disciples preached the Word of God, but they also operated in signs, wonders, and miracles through the power of the Holy Spirit. In 1 Corinthians 2:4-5, the Apostle Paul said, "And my speech and my preaching was not with enticing words of man's wisdom, but in demonstration of the Spirit and of power: that your faith should not stand in the wisdom of men, but in the power of God."

Paul preached the gospel to people in Ephesus. In Acts 19, when Paul prayed with the people, they received the Holy Spirit and spoke in tongues. Verses 1-6 say,

> *And it came to pass, that, while Apollos was at Corinth, Paul having passed through the upper coasts came to Ephesus: and finding certain disciples, he said unto them, Have ye received the Holy Ghost since ye believed? And they said unto him, We have not so much as heard whether there be any Holy Ghost. And he said unto them, Unto what then were ye baptized? And they said, Unto John's baptism. Then said Paul, John verily baptized with the baptism of repentance, saying unto the people, that they should believe on him which should come after him, that is, on Christ Jesus. When they heard this, they were baptized in the name of the Lord Jesus. And when Paul had laid his hands upon them, the Holy Ghost came on them; and they spake with tongues, and prophesied.*

Because many churches do not preach the baptism of the Holy Spirit evidenced by speaking in tongues, people often are like the disciples in Ephesus who had not "heard whether there be any Holy Ghost." When Paul prayed for them, the

Holy Ghost came on them, and they spoke in tongues and prophesied. Have you been filled with the baptism of the Holy Ghost? Have you received dunamis Holy Ghost power, or are you in a power blackout and don't even know it?

The coming Great Awakening is more than a revival. It is a widespread, sweeping movement that will affect more than just one city or region. The effects of this move of God are far-reaching and will touch and impact many segments of society. Revivals and movements of God have come in waves ever since the Azusa Street Revival in 1906. Azusa Street is probably the greatest revival the world has ever seen—apart from the day of Pentecost.

It amazes me how many Spirit-filled, tongue-talking, born-again Christians don't know the history of the Pentecostal/Charismatic Movement. The defining characteristic of Pentecostal revival is the baptism of the Holy Spirit evidenced by speaking in tongues. However, today many Spirit-filled Pentecostal and charismatic churches don't even preach about this experience. The seeker-friendly approach ("Let's not scare the visitors") has led to a watering down in our churches. When was the last time you attended a service in which an altar call was given for Holy Spirit baptism seekers? When was the last time you saw someone receive the baptism of the Holy Spirit? How many people do you know, either in church or out of church, who do not speak in tongues?

Many pastors today have decided that speaking in tongues is optional and should not be pushed on a person. We all know that the gospel message is received according to the seeker's free will. A person has the right to accept or reject the gospel, but how can we call ourselves Spirit-filled if we withhold from others this message of power that has transformed our lives?

Come, Holy Spirit

Is the Holy Spirit welcome in your church? I have had people attend our church and say that there is too much talk here about the Holy Spirit. "We don't want to hear about it, and we don't want to receive the baptism of the Holy Spirit." What is a pastor to do? Compromise? Are we supposed to kick the Holy Spirit out the door to make people feel comfortable?

I know that we cannot force Holy Spirit baptism on people, but we cannot force salvation on people either. Either they receive it or they don't. Whatever people decide, we *cannot* and *will not* change the gospel message! I have seen more than one person walk out of our church doors, not to return, because they were offended by the Holy Spirit.

Did you know that the Bible says that Jesus offended people? Did you know that the gospel offends people? If people are offended, think about the source of the offense, which is our Lord Himself. When I see people walk out of our church because they were offended by the Holy Spirit, all I can say is, "Thank you, Jesus," because I will *never* compromise or grieve the Holy Spirit in our church!

When I think back on all those years ago in 1990 when God filled me with the Holy Spirit, I wonder. I wonder, "What if the pastor of that church had told his people that prayer only happens in a back room before service? What if he had said that nobody is allowed to speak in tongues during service? What if he said, 'Don't get too wild during worship; it might scare the visitors'? What if he said, 'Holy Spirit baptism is optional; you can pray for it if you want, but it's not really a big deal'?"

Would I be Spirit-filled today if that pastor restricted his service? Thank God for those people who were not ashamed or afraid to let the Holy Spirit control that church! You see, the

Holy Spirit is a big deal. He's a HUGE deal! When I received the baptism of the Holy Spirit, I began a brand new life. What kind of a hypocrite would I be if I allowed the devil to shut my mouth and not tell others about the most powerful experience they can receive in their life?

We are all praying and believing God for revival (which I believe has already started), but we cannot leave out the key ingredient—the baptism of the Holy Spirit!

Would you like to receive the power of the Holy Ghost? Ask and believe God to fill you with Holy Ghost power!

Chapter 9: Get into the River

Everything blossoms in springtime, but sunlight and water are needed for plants to grow. The more it rains, the faster things grow. Water is necessary for life. Because there is no water in a desert, you find nothing but sand and maybe a cactus. Where there is no water, nothing grows. Some of you may feel that your life is like a desert. If you feel that you are in a dry and weary land, there is hope. Isaiah 35:7 says, "And the parched ground shall become a pool, and the thirsty land springs of water: in the habitation of dragons, where each lay, shall be grass with reeds and rushes."

Any farmer knows that if it does not rain, the crops will not grow. When there is a drought, all living things suffer. Plants cannot grow and animals cannot drink water. We must have water to live. When we are thirsty, what is the first thing we want to do? Take a drink of water. Water is refreshing and takes away our thirst. Our physical bodies need water, but the Bible tells us about spiritual water. What is spiritual water? Isaiah 44:3-4 says, "For I will pour water upon him that is thirsty, and floods upon the dry ground: I will pour my spirit upon thy seed, and my blessing upon thine offspring: and they shall spring up as among the grass, as willows by the water courses."

In John chapter 4, Jesus had a conversation with a woman about spiritual, or living, water. He told her that anyone who drinks water will thirst again, but whoever drinks living water will never thirst again. Are you thirsty? Not for a drink of water, but for spiritual water. Do you need a drink of living water? Do you need the baptism of the Holy Spirit which will satisfy your spiritual thirst? Jesus explained that living water is the Holy Spirit. John 7:37-39 says,

> *In the last day, that great day of the feast, Jesus stood and cried, saying, If any man thirst, let him come unto me, and drink. He that believeth on me, as the scripture hath said, out of his belly shall flow rivers of living water. (But this spake he of the Spirit, which they that believe on him should receive: for the Holy Ghost was not yet given; because that Jesus was not yet glorified.)*

If you would like a drink of living water right now, if you need a touch of the Holy Spirit, raise your hands and begin to praise Him. You will feel His presence. It is refreshing to take a drink of cold water. Swimming is also very enjoyable. In the summertime, you will find children laughing and splashing around in the pool. Most children love to be in the water, but sometimes you see a child standing on the side of the pool, afraid to get in. The child may stick a toe in the water, but that's all. One can only assume that the child doesn't know how to swim or is afraid of the water.

The Holy Spirit is living water. We drink of this water when we receive the baptism of the Holy Spirit. The Spirit is refreshing, like swimming in a pool, but some people are like the child who sits by the side of the water, afraid to get in. Some people don't understand the joy, peace, love, and power that the Holy Spirit gives. For whatever reason, they don't want to get into the water of life. Have you gotten into the river or are you still on the side? Are you enjoying all that God has for you or do you hold back? Are you hot, tired, and thirsty? It's time to jump into the river of God and be refreshed! Everything you need can be found in the river of God. It is refreshing and healing. Stop holding back because it's time to get into the river of God!

In 2006, too much rain caused the rivers to crest their banks and flood Lake County, Ohio. The flooding destroyed many homes and caused many people to suffer. There were many stories of people leaving their houses in the middle of the night with nothing but the clothes on their backs. Some people had to find a new place to live.

We don't want a flood like that to happen again, but God wants to pour out a flood of the Holy Spirit in this area. A flood of the Spirit refreshes and brings life. We need a mighty outpouring of the Holy Spirit! We want God to send a spiritual flood! We want people to be filled with the Holy Spirit!

An outpouring of the Spirit brings revival. If you are filled with the Holy Spirit, you already have the living water. Let the Spirit flow in your life! Let the river flow! In the Bible, there was a drought and famine in the land, but Elijah saw the rain coming. In 1 Kings 18:41-45 it says,

> *And Elijah said unto Ahab, Get thee up, eat and drink; for there is a sound of abundance of rain. So Ahab went up to eat and to drink. And Elijah went up to the top of Carmel; and he cast himself down upon the earth, and put his face between his knees, and said to his servant, Go up now, look toward the sea. And he went up, and looked, and said, There is nothing. And he said, Go again seven times. And it came to pass at the seventh time, that he said, Behold, there ariseth a little cloud out of the sea,*

like a man's hand. And he said, Go up, say unto Ahab, Prepare thy chariot, and get thee down that the rain stop thee not. And it came to pass in the mean while, that the heaven was black with clouds and wind, and there was a great rain. And Ahab rode, and went to Jezreel.

I am here today to declare to this city that the drought is over! It is time for the rain to fall! It is time for a flood of the Holy Spirit! It's time for God's people to get into the river! Lord Jesus, send a flood of the Spirit like we have never seen! Fill souls with Your Spirit!

Chapter 10: The Glory Cloud

In the Old Testament, God delivered His people Israel from slavery in Egypt. God used Moses to lead the people out by performing signs and wonders. God delivered His people with a mighty hand and an outstretched arm. Deuteronomy 26:8- 9 says, "And the Lord brought us forth out of Egypt with a mighty hand, and with an outstretched arm, and with great terribleness, and with signs, and with wonders: and he hath brought us into this place, and hath given us this land, even a land that floweth with milk and honey."

Only after ten plagues did Pharaoh release the children of Israel. After they left Egypt, Pharaoh decided to chase them. God opened the Red Sea so the Israelites could pass through, but then He closed it and caused the Egyptian army to drown. After they crossed the Red Sea, God led the Israelites through the wilderness on the way to the Promised Land. God's presence went before them, revealed as a pillar of a cloud by day and a pillar of fire by night (Exodus 13:21-22).

God has different ways of manifesting Himself. He used a cloud to reveal His presence to Israel. A word often used to refer to the presence, or glory, of God is *shekinah*. The *shekinah* glory of God is where His presence dwells, in the glory cloud. When Moses and the children of Israel reached Mt. Sinai, God manifested His presence to the people. Exodus 24:15-18 says,

And Moses went up into the mount, and a cloud covered the mount. And the glory of the Lord abode upon mount Sinai, and the cloud covered it six days: and the seventh day he called unto Moses out of the midst of the cloud. And the sight of the glory of the Lord was like devouring fire on the top of the mount in the eyes of the children of Israel. And Moses went into the midst of the cloud, and gat him up into the mount: and Moses was in the mount forty days and forty nights.

When Moses came down from the mountain, his face was shining. This can happen to us today, when we come into the presence of the Lord. A woman, who was hunched over and appeared sad, came into a Bible study I was teaching. We began to pray, and I asked her to lift up her hands and reach out to the Lord. As she prayed, the Lord began to move, and she was touched. When we were done praying, her whole countenance had totally changed. She no longer looked sad, but uplifted; her face was shining! I have seen other people with shining, glowing faces. This happens when the glory, or the presence, of God is on them.

The shekinah glory cloud can appear today. The presence of God was evident during the evening service of a church conference I attended, and many people were touched. The next day, people began testifying about the service. They said that in the front of the church toward the ceiling, they saw the glory cloud. For the rest of the conference, I kept my eyes on the spot where they saw the cloud! God instructed Israel to build a tabernacle in the wilderness. God's presence would dwell in the tabernacle where the people worshipped and made sacrifices. The glory cloud filled the tabernacle. Exodus 40:34-35 says: "Then a cloud covered the tent of the congregation, and the glory of the Lord filled the tabernacle. And Moses was not able to enter into the tent of the congregation, because the cloud abode thereon, and the glory of the Lord filled the tabernacle."

After the Israelites entered the Promised Land, kings ruled over them. King David was a man after God's heart, and God blessed him greatly. David wanted to build a temple unto the Lord in Jerusalem, but his son, King Solomon, completed the task. When the temple was dedicated, the people worshipped, and the glory of the Lord filled the temple (2 Chronicles 5:13-14).

I have been at church services where the praise and worship was so high that the glory of God came and took over the service. As I've mentioned, I call this a Holy Ghost takeover. When this happens, God begins to move and minister to the people. Some people dance and worship the Lord with all their might. Others fall face down at the altar, and some bow before the Lord. God Himself directs the altar call. Everyone in the church reaches out to the Lord in some way. The preacher does not preach. Everyone prays—some with their hands lifted up to God. Some people weep and others shake. Some call out while others speak in tongues. Praise and worship is very important in a church service because it ushers in the presence, or glory, of God. When the glory of God comes in, things begin to happen. People can be healed in their seats. Miracles take place. King David danced before the Lord with all his might (2 Samuel 6:14-15).

I grew up in a church that did not teach the baptism of the Holy Spirit. People worshipped quietly. No one clapped their hands, or shouted, or danced. When I came to a Pentecostal church, it was very different. People worshipped out loud, often standing with their hands raised. Some spoke in tongues. I felt something in this church that I had never felt before—

the Holy Spirit. I was told that I could pray to be filled with the Holy Spirit with the evidence of speaking in tongues. When God filled me with the baptism of the Holy Spirit, I felt joy that I had never known before. I understood why people would jump, run, shout, laugh, dance, and clap their hands. I understood what it meant to be slain in the Spirit. Some think that people in a Pentecostal church service are just being emotional. I do get emotional when I think about the goodness of the Lord! I've had joy, peace, and love since Jesus came into my life. I want to worship the Lord with my whole heart. There is nothing wrong with getting excited about God! People go to sports games and scream and behave passionately. They are called fans. But when we do it in church, we are called fanatics! I have no problem being a fanatic for Jesus!

Do you want to feel the joy of the Lord? Do you need the presence and glory of God? Then worship the Lord with your whole heart. If you want to feel the presence of the Lord, begin to praise Him. He can supply your every need as you worship Him. Some people say that there is a dark cloud over us. I know that the *shekinah* glory cloud can remove any dark cloud! Let's praise the Lord and thank Him for the glory cloud coming into this city! Lord, we ask that Your glory would fill us like it filled the temple! Let Your glory come and fill this place!

Chapter 11: The Party is Here

After Jesus was resurrected from the dead, He appeared to His disciples many times. When He ascended into heaven, He gave them instructions to go into Jerusalem and wait for the promise of the Holy Spirit. The disciples were all with one accord in one place. On the day of Pentecost, the Holy Spirit was poured out in the upper room in Jerusalem. The people who heard the disciples speaking in tongues were confused. They even accused them of being drunk.

The Bible compares the Holy Spirit to new wine. Have you ever seen a person who is drunk? Or someone high on drugs? Anyone who has experienced being drunk on alcohol knows that their mood heightens and their inhibitions lower. Under the influence, people talk louder, become friendlier, and may even start dancing. They don't worry about what other people might think about them at that moment. Alcohol is served at some parties to loosen up the crowd, to break the ice. Have you ever attended a Holy Ghost party? Why don't you take a drink of Holy Ghost new wine and loosen up right now? There ain't no party like a Holy Ghost party, and the Holy Ghost party never stops!

When the Holy Spirit comes into our lives, He brings us joy, peace, and love. Romans 14:17 says, "For the kingdom of God is not meat and drink; but righteousness, and peace, and joy in the Holy Ghost." Some churches are so dead, dry, cold, and depressing that you feel like grabbing the microphone to ask the frozen chosen, "Who died? Let's get this party started! Break out the Holy Ghost new wine!"

In the 1990s, a revivalist named Rodney Howard-Browne traveled around America throwing Holy Ghost parties. At his services, people would start to laugh for no apparent reason and behave as though happily drunk. He became known as the Holy Ghost bartender. We were having revival meetings a couple of years ago and the guest speaker began to pray for people. When he laid his hands on them, they began to laugh. He laid hands on me, and I immediately fell down to the floor and laughed uncontrollably! The Holy Spirit was flowing in that service, and joy was being poured out!

Many people today are afraid. They are searching for a sense of safety and security. Many people feel an emptiness inside that they try to fill with different things. Two of satan's major strongholds are inferiority and insecurity. Many Christians don't know their identity in Christ, and they continue to define themselves based on who they were in the past. What we need is a good dose of the Holy Ghost! Anybody need a drink right now? Get out your Holy Ghost wine glass and let's have a drink! Lord, give us a drink of new wine! After a couple of drinks, everything starts to look better!

Ephesians 5:18 says, "And be not drunk with wine, wherein is excess; but be filled with the Spirit." My name is Melinda Bauman, and I am a Holy Ghost drunk! I confess to frequently drinking new wine and being under the influence! Actually, I could use a drink right now! I have found that preaching is much easier when you are drunk on the Holy Ghost! Fill my cup, Lord! More, Lord!

Melinda Bauman

Holy laughter is a controversial manifestation of the Holy Spirit in revival meetings. What is wrong with being happy and joyful? People laughing in church can't be of God? Would you rather be sad and depressed? What do happy people often do? They laugh! People who are experiencing holy laughter are filled with the joy of the Lord. We have had services where holy laughter broke out and took over the whole meeting. Some people may think it is disruptive, an interruption to the service. Who would you rather be in charge of the service, God or man? Psalm 126:2-3 says, "Then was our mouth filled with laughter, and our tongue with singing: then said they among the heathen, The Lord hath done great things for them. The Lord hath done great things for us; whereof we are glad."

When the holy laughter broke out at our service, the guest speaker realized he would not be able to finish his sermon. Suddenly he was slain in the Spirit and fell on the floor! He stayed down for a few minutes and could not get back up. God moved in that service. Many people received prayer and were touched by the Holy Spirit. After the service was over, the speaker finally got up and appeared somewhat drunk!

A revivalist came to our church and asked the question, "Are you sure you want revival? Because when revival breaks out, the Holy Spirit will be in control." Not all pastors are willing to give up control in their church. The revivalist said revival broke out once when he was preaching. After the service, he was escorted into the pastor's office and told that he would not be welcome back to that church!

When the Holy Spirit moves, unpredictable things happen. I have no desire to bring the Holy Spirit under my control. God is a God of order, but it is not the order of straight rows and predictable church services. When the Holy Spirit is in charge, you may get out at noon and you may not. You may hear two sermons that day or you may hear none; there may be an altar call that looks like chaos.

We must allow the Holy Spirit to work in our services; we cannot be too in control to accommodate God's will. The Holy Spirit must have the freedom to move in our churches. We cannot put God on a timetable or dictate when He can have His way. Are you flexible enough to handle the new wine? In the Bible, Jesus offended religious leaders. They represented the old wineskins, and Jesus was bringing new wine.

Whenever revival breaks out, the old wineskins oppose the new wine. The people who were satisfied with the revivals of the past will not want to drink the new wine. Some people who attended the Toronto Revival or the Brownsville Revival in the 1990s are not looking for revival today. They just talk about how great revival was back then. They do not seem to want revival or care if it happens again.

But the Holy Spirit knows how to make even the old wineskins hunger and thirst for more of God. The Lord knows how to challenge them to come and drink, to "taste and see that the Lord is good" (Psalm 34:8). Don't force people to come to revival meetings against their will; just shine all the brighter so that your joy will create a thirst in them for the wine you're drinking!

Chapter 12: Understanding the Anointing

Jesus is the Son of God. He is God made manifest in the flesh for the salvation of the world. In the Gospels, Jesus made it clear that He came to do the will of the Father. Jesus' ministry included supernatural healing and miracles. Everywhere He went, He healed the sick, cast out devils, and performed miracles. Many people believed in Him because of the works that He did. Crowds followed Him everywhere He went.

While He was on earth, Jesus preached the gospel and was anointed with the power of the Holy Ghost. What is the anointing? In the Old Testament, anointing oil was used to consecrate kings and priests. Whenever someone was chosen for an office, they were anointed with oil. The oil was a symbol of dedication for service. The anointing oil represents sanctification. Jesus explained why He was anointed in Luke 4:18-19: "The Spirit of the Lord is upon me, because he hath anointed me to preach the gospel to the poor; he hath sent me to heal the brokenhearted, to preach deliverance to the captives, and recovering of sight to the blind, to set at liberty them that are bruised, to preach the acceptable year of the Lord."

Jesus Christ came to bring salvation, healing, and deliverance to the people. Jesus was a great miracle worker; He caused the blind to see, the deaf to hear, and the lame to walk.

Christos, or *Christ,* is a Greek word meaning "anointed."[5] When we say Jesus Christ, we are saying Jesus the Anointed One. In the Old Testament, when oil was poured upon kings and priests, they were consecrated, or dedicated, to God's service. The oil symbolized a new anointing, a new level of responsibility, and a new outpouring on the life of the person being anointed. The anointing is the supernatural enablement of God which He gives to a person through the Holy Spirit to accomplish His purposes. This anointing is available to all believers today who want to fulfill God's will for their lives.

God gave Moses instructions for preparing the anointing oil and rules regarding its use. Exodus 30:25-30 says,

> *And thou shalt make it an oil of holy ointment, an ointment compound after the art of the apothecary: it shall be an holy anointing oil. And thou shalt anoint the tabernacle of the congregation therewith, and the ark of the testimony. And the table and all his vessels, and the candlestick and his vessels, and the altar of incense, and the altar of burnt offering with all his vessels, and the laver and his foot. And thou shalt sanctify them, that they may be most holy: whatsoever toucheth them shall be holy. And thou shalt anoint Aaron and his sons, and consecrate them, that they may minister unto me in the priest's office.*

When someone is anointed by God, they are set apart for God's service. The anointing releases supernatural power to do those things that we cannot do in our own strength or

---

5. Thayer and Smith, "Greek Lexicon entry for Christos," The NAS New Testament Greek Lexicon, http://www.biblestudytools.com/lexicons/greek/nas/christos.html (accessed April 16, 2014).

abilities. The Old Testament priests were anointed before they could serve in their offices. Anointing was the first ceremony in the inauguration of Jewish kings. The anointing of kings and priests signified the influence of the Holy Spirit on their lives.

Sometimes supernatural anointing oil can manifest a fragrant odor in church services. This has happened in our church. Here are some testimonies from some of the brethren in our church regarding this:

"When we are free in our worship to God, He shows up in many ways—with His healing power, with His joy, and with His deliverance for His people. But how unique was our worship today? The beautiful smell, the lovely fragrance of His very own presence for our natural senses to enjoy! At first I smelled it without thinking too much about it. Then another person from the back spoke it out loud. What a combination of sweetness and goodness in the smell! Then the girl behind me and I both smelled it. The worship was so beautiful. We looked at the oil bottles in the church, only to find they were not open. I thank the Lord for what I believe was a wonder He bestowed upon us today in worship."

"While worshipping Jesus, suddenly I smelled a fragrance floating by me. It seemed to float by me from behind, crossing over to the right side. The scent lasted a few seconds. It was like a cool, light smell. I thought it was someone's cologne. I continued worshipping and didn't say anything. When the worship service ended, a woman sitting in front of me said she smelled oil. I said that I also smelled it, and at the same time a man in the back said he also smelled oil! No one was wearing any cologne or perfume."

"During worship, I was walking around in the back of the room. I smelled oil, and it had such a strong scent. I looked around and said, 'Does anybody else smell this?' I could smell it from the front to the back. The Lord said to me, 'FRESH OIL.' He said He was pouring it out, and the fragrance was really strong. One of the ladies said that she smelled the oil too. There is oil on the front table in the church, but the bottles were not opened. The fragrance smelled like myrrh mixed with different spices. There was such a sweetness and fragrance of God's love and His Spirit among us."

When Christians receive the baptism of the Holy Spirit, evidenced by speaking in tongues, we also receive the anointing of God. In the Old Testament, only certain people, such as kings and priests, were anointed. In the New Testament, all Spirit-filled Christians are anointed. We are referred to as a royal priesthood in 1 Peter 2:9: "But ye are a chosen generation, a royal priesthood, an holy nation, a peculiar people; that ye should shew forth the praises of him who hath called you out of darkness into his marvelous light."

We must operate in the anointing of the Holy Spirit if we expect to do the works that Jesus called us to do: preach the gospel, heal the sick, raise the dead, and cast out devils. We cannot do the work of the ministry in our own strength; if we could, we wouldn't need the anointing. We are anointed with the oil of the Holy Spirit when we receive the baptism of the Holy Spirit, but God can also anoint us with fresh oil.

We can receive fresh oil and also new oil. When God takes what we already have and makes it fresh again, we have been anointed with fresh oil; we already have that spiritual gift. When we start operating in a spiritual gift that we've never operated in before, we have received new oil. For example, a person with the prophetic gift can receive fresh oil and operate in a greater level of prophecy. When we get new oil, we receive spiritual gifts that are new to us, such as the gifts of miracles and healing. Many Christians want anointing and power to come upon their lives in areas where they never had power before. Psalm 92:10 says, "But my horn shalt thou exalt like the horn of an unicorn: I shall be anointed with fresh oil."

The first thing we must do before we can receive fresh oil is be consecrated to the Lord in a lifestyle of holiness. The word *anoint* means "to rub and smear."[6] God wants to anoint us with His power and His presence. You have to seek the face of God for the anointing. It will cost us everything. Moving in the anointing always involves the unknown. We have to be willing to step out in faith and exercise the gifts that the Holy Spirit gives us.

Jesus Christ had an anointing for healing. When He laid hands on people, or even when someone touched His clothes, they were made whole. Peter also operated in the anointing of healing. Peter carried such a great anointing that when people brought the sick out onto the streets, Acts tells us that his shadow would heal them. The shadow is the presence of the Holy Spirit.

The power of God to heal is tangible and transferable. The laying on of hands is not just a point of contact for faith. It's the way the tangible Spirit of God gets transferred to someone. Peter and John had the anointing of healing and prayed for a lame man in Acts 3:1-8:

6. The American Heritage® Dictionary of the English Language, Fourth Edition. S.v. "anoint." Retrieved April 16 2014 from http://www.thefreedictionary.com/anoint.

Come, Holy Spirit

Now Peter and John went up together into the temple at the hour of prayer, being the ninth hour. And a certain man lame from his mother's womb was carried, whom they laid daily at the gate of the temple which is called Beautiful, to ask alms of them that entered into the temple; who seeing Peter and John about to go into the temple asked an alms. And Peter, fastening his eyes upon him with John, said, Look on us. And he gave heed unto them, expecting to receive something of them. Then Peter said, Silver and gold have I none; but such as I have give I thee: In the name of Jesus Christ of Nazareth rise up and walk. And he took him by the right hand, and lifted him up: and immediately his feet and ankle bones received strength. And he leaping up stood, and walked, and entered with them into the temple, walking, and leaping, and praising God.

Let's seek the Lord for more anointing (fresh oil and new oil): *God, we want more of the anointing, whatever the cost. We want more of the Holy Spirit to come upon our lives. Anoint us with Your oil and use us as vessels for Your glory, in the name of Jesus.*

Chapter 13: The Shaking

There is a shaking taking place in America. What happens when something gets shaken? It causes a change, or a shift. When a person is shaken, something dramatic happens to them. People can be shaken when a loud noise wakes them out of their sleep. People notice when there is a shaking going on; it gets their attention. There are shakings in the physical world and in the spiritual world. Many times what happens in the natural world is a reflection of something happening in the spirit world. An example of a shaking in the natural world is an earthquake. In the Bible, earthquakes were the result of something that happened in the spiritual realm. Let's read about an earthquake in Acts 16:25-30:

And at midnight Paul and Silas prayed, and sang praises unto God: and the prisoners heard them. And suddenly there was a great earthquake, so that the foundations of the prison were shaken: and immediately all the doors were opened, and every one's bands were loosed. And the keeper of the prison awaking out of his sleep, and seeing the prison doors open, he drew out his sword, and would have killed himself, supposing that the prisoners had been fled. But Paul cried with a loud voice, saying, Do thyself no harm: for we are all here. Then he called for a light, and sprang in,

*and came trembling, and fell down before Paul
and Silas, and brought them out, and said, Sirs,
what must I do to be saved?*

When there is a shaking in the natural, it can cause an
awakening in the spiritual. Paul and Silas were thrown into
prison because they preached the gospel. Instead of getting
upset, they spent their time in prison praying and singing
praises to God. God heard them and caused an earthquake
which opened the prison doors. The guard was so shaken that
he wanted to get saved. When the saints pray, God moves. Peter
was thrown into prison in Acts 12, but as the people of God
were praying, an angel was sent to release Peter from prison.

Perhaps something upsetting has happened in your life
recently. Instead of getting angry and upset, pray and praise
God in the midst of your circumstance. God sent an angel to
open the prison doors for Peter. Begin to praise God in spite of
your situation, and see what God will do for you! Let's begin
to praise Him right now. There were other times in the Bible
when a shaking occurred. Let's look again at Acts 2:1-4:

*And when the day of Pentecost was fully come,
they were all with one accord in one place. And
suddenly there came a sound from heaven as of
a rushing mighty wind, and it filled all the house
where they were sitting. And there appeared unto
them cloven tongues like as of fire, and it sat upon
each of them. And they were all filled with the Holy
Ghost, and began to speak with other tongues, as
the Spirit gave them utterance.*

This passage is about the outpouring of the Holy Ghost on the day of Pentecost. There was a sound from heaven as of a rushing mighty wind, and it filled the whole house. When the Spirit was poured out, the people were filled and spoke in tongues. This shaking began the New Testament church. Before Jesus ascended into heaven, He told His followers to go wait in Jerusalem for the promise of the Holy Spirit. Before the outpouring of the Spirit, the people were praying. What was the result of the day of Pentecost? People were saved. On the day that Peter preached the first sermon of the early church, three thousand souls were saved.

What causes a shaking or revival? Prayer. What is the result of revival? Souls are saved. One of the worst natural disasters in the 1900s was the San Francisco earthquake. This earthquake happened on April 18, 1906, and it ranks as one of the most significant earthquakes of all time. The earthquake was felt from southern Oregon to south of Los Angeles and inland as far as Nevada. Even though the shaking damage was equally severe in many places, the earthquake was best remembered for the fire that destroyed San Francisco.

What else happened in California that same year? On April 14, 1906, a group of Christians met at the Azusa Street Mission in Los Angeles. They were filled with the Holy Spirit, evidenced by speaking in tongues. The worship at the Azusa Street Revival was frequent and spontaneous, with services going on twenty-four hours a day. People came from all over the world to receive their Pentecostal experience. What has been called the "world's greatest revival" resulted in an army of six hundred million Spirit-filled believers touching every nation on earth.

A 2007 article, "Quake Shakes Up Lake County," said that a minor earthquake shook the central and western portions of

Lake County, Ohio, on October 17. Preliminary results show
the earthquake occurred northwest of Mentor-on-the-Lake
in Lake Erie and reached a magnitude of 3.0. Earthquakes
registering less than a magnitude of 3.5 are not generally
felt, but are recorded, according to seismologists. But after
the quake hit, police and fire departments were flooded with
calls. The Lake County area recorded 14 earthquakes in 2006.
Small earthquakes in recent years have escalated in the area,
and scientists are not sure why. The most severe was in June
2007 near Painesville and had a magnitude of 3.8.[7]

There is a shaking taking place in America. Many people
today would say that we are living in perilous times. Many in
our country are fearful and uncertain about their future. Ever
since the year 2000, America has had challenging times. This
last decade has been difficult, and people are wondering if God
has forsaken this country. In 2001, Muslim terrorists attacked
America. In 2003, America went to war with Iraq. After that,
the economy declined as the dollar lost value and jobs moved
overseas. In 2006, the real estate market declined and houses
went into foreclosure. Then the stock market collapsed and
since 2008, America has been in a recession.

Throughout history, there have been dark periods as
well as times of revival. Revivals occur in times of moral
darkness and national depression. They begin in the hearts of
God's people. There must be an increase in prayer, fasting,
repentance, and a burden to see souls saved. A great revival is
coming. Before this revival happens, there will be a shaking.
As saints of God, what can we do to help bring about this
revival? Pray. What will be the result? Many souls will be

7. Jeffrey L Frischkorn, "Quake Shakes Up Lake County," The News-Herald, October 18, 2007.

saved. Do you need boldness? Do what the early Christians did in Acts 4:29-31:

> *And now, Lord, behold their threatenings: and grant unto thy servants, that with all boldness they may speak thy word, by stretching forth thine hand to heal; and that signs and wonders may be done by the name of thy holy child Jesus. And when they had prayed, the place was shaken where they were assembled together; and they were all filled with the Holy Ghost, and they spake the word of God with boldness.*

When the saints of God are filled with Holy Ghost boldness, they are not afraid to reach out to the Lord in faith. The believers in the book of Acts performed healings, miracles, signs, and wonders.

There is a shaking coming to America. Revival is coming to our cities. People will be shaken, and they will turn to the Lord. This will bring about a shift in this country. Just as there was a shaking in California in 1906, there is a shaking going on today. The end result will be a mighty move of God, and many souls will be saved. Are you ready for this end-time revival? Do you want to be part of it? Are you praying and seeking the Lord? Do you have Holy Ghost boldness? Are you ready to do the works of Jesus? In Matthew 10:7-8 Jesus said, "And as ye go, preach, saying, The kingdom of heaven is at hand. Heal the sick, cleanse the lepers, raise the dead, cast out devils: freely ye have received, freely give."

Revival begins in the church. If you want a fresh touch of the power of God, if you need boldness; if you want to be used by God, then ask Him for it.

Chapter 14: Are You a Soul Winner?

Jesus Christ is the Son of God who came to earth to save the lost. He came to die for our sins so that we could have eternal life. Jesus came to present the kingdom of heaven—the gospel message of salvation, healing, and deliverance. In order to fulfill the requirements for salvation, Jesus gave His own life on the cross. His blood was shed as a sacrifice to take away the sins of the world. After He died, He was buried and then rose from the dead.

Jesus had twelve disciples and many followers in the Bible. The disciples were expected to forsake all to follow Him; many of them were fishermen. When Jesus called the disciples, they were busy fishing. But when Jesus said, "Follow Me and I will make you fishers of men," they dropped everything and followed Him. Matthew 4:18-22 says,

> *And Jesus, walking by the sea of Galilee, saw two brethren, Simon called Peter, and Andrew his brother, casting a net into the sea: for they were fishers. And he saith unto them, Follow me, and I will make you fishers of men. And they straightway left their nets, and followed him. And going on from thence, he saw other two brethren, James the son of Zebedee, and John his brother, in a ship with Zebedee their father, mending their nets; and*

he called them. And they immediately left the ship and their father, and followed him.

What does it mean to be fishers of men? For the disciples, it meant that they would become soul winners. Jesus is our primary example of a soul winner, because He came to save sinners by dying on the cross for our salvation. Jesus died for the sins of the world and He gave His life willingly.

Jesus shed His blood and died so that our sins could be forgiven and we could be healed. Everything available from Jesus was made possible because of His blood. Salvation, healing, and deliverance are made possible through the shed blood of Jesus. This is why He died for you and me. Because we are sinners, we have been doomed to spiritual death. But Jesus died in our place so that we can have eternal life. Only Jesus could pay the price for our sins. Jesus laid down His life so we can have eternal life.

As disciples of Jesus Christ, it is our commission to tell people what Jesus did for us and lead them to accept Him as their Savior. The only way for our sins to be forgiven is through the blood the Jesus. When we accept Jesus into our lives and ask for forgiveness, His blood washes away our sins.

When Jesus healed the sick, gave sight to the blind, and fed the people fishes and loaves of bread, great crowds followed Him. Many people followed Him because of the miracles He performed. Jesus told the fishermen who became His disciples to follow Him so they could become fishers of men.

What is a disciple? A disciple is a follower of Jesus Christ. Once you receive salvation and become a Christian, you are a disciple. What does it take to be a disciple of Jesus Christ? A disciple is expected to forsake all to follow Jesus just as the

Twelve He called in the Gospels did. A disciple is expected to be a soul winner just like Jesus was.

When I stepped out in ministry and began holding weekly Bible studies, I quickly learned that it was a lot of work, requiring a lot of time and commitment. I prayed and asked God to motivate me, to give me a reason to do ministry. He spoke two things that I will always remember: 1) Do ministry because you love God, and 2) Do ministry because you love people. A minister must have a vision. Without vision, people perish. When we began holding monthly revival services, the vision was twofold: 1) Invite speakers who demonstrate the power of God, and 2) Train and equip the church to operate in the power of God.

Jesus had many followers. When He healed the sick, performed miracles, and fed the people, great crowds followed Him. Many people followed Him because of the miracles He performed, but not as many were willing to be His disciples. Here at our church, we hold special revival meetings and invite speakers who operate in the spiritual gifts. The prophetic and healing services draw crowds of people who come to receive ministry. Many people come, but few people stay and make a commitment to serve in the church and become soul winners.

Jesus had many followers, but only a few disciples were willing to surrender everything in order to serve Him. Which one are you? Are you a follower who comes to church just to receive something from God, or are you a disciple who wants to be a committed and faithful servant of God? The Bible says not to pray for the harvest, for the harvest is already ripe. We are to pray for laborers to work in the harvest field.

Jesus loves sinners and came to die on the cross for them. Even though He loves sinners, He expects them to change. Jesus was sent to the weak, the oppressed, and the sinners. The Pharisees were very upset when Jesus spent time with sinners.

A big percentage of the world's population—billions of souls alive today—have never heard the gospel. Time is slipping away for many people in this world. About two people in the world die every second, one hundred people each minute, and fifty million people each year. Most of them are dying without Christ in their lives. Do you have a burden for lost souls? It is the call and duty of every born-again believer to share the gospel of Jesus Christ. Witnessing is not only for pastors and evangelists. Are you saved? Then it is your responsibility too. The world is dying and going to hell.

A church survey asks the question: "Why did you visit our church?" Eighty percent of the people said they came because a friend or relative invited them. Do you have any friends or relatives who are not saved and do not go to church? Have you ever witnessed to them or invited them to church?

When we invite people to church who we know personally, they will often come because we have a relationship with them. All Christians, not just the pastor, should witness and invite people to come to church. Start off with your friends, relatives, and neighbors. After that, it will be easier to ask people you see occasionally—like the cashier at the bank or the man at the gas station.

If unsaved people are not coming into the church, we have to go out and witness to them where they are. How do we witness to people? One of the most powerful ways is to give your personal salvation testimony. People nowadays are stressed about the recession and are struggling financially.

You could offer to pray with people who need a job or some financial breakthrough.

God can use our spiritual gifts to help us evangelize people on the streets or wherever we meet them. Prophetic evangelism occurs when God gives us a word to minister to someone. Many people are sick and need prayer for healing. I have rarely met a person who turned down my offer to pray for their healing, and most are grateful when you do pray. After we pray for someone's healing or give them a prophetic word, we can ask if they know Jesus as their Savior. They may give their lives to the Lord on the spot and they may be willing to come to church if you invite them.

Do you feel called into the ministry? All Christians are called to do the ministry of Jesus which includes preaching the gospel to the lost and making disciples. I began in the ministry by teaching Bible studies out of a coffeehouse. I had a desire to witness to people as an outreach of the church. A coffeehouse is a neutral location where people who may not be ready to come into a church would be willing to go. Many people came to the Bible studies, and some did eventually come to the church.

I was teaching a home Bible study to a married couple. I was in their home praying for the wife. Suddenly, something in the Spirit hit me, and I knew I needed to ask this woman about her issues with anxiety. So I asked her if something was troubling her; she confirmed that there was. I didn't understand how I could know that; then God showed me that He was using me to help her. The couple's daughter came to church, and God filled her with the Holy Spirit. Thank You, Jesus.

I was teaching a home Bible study to a Catholic woman, who was receptive to the Holy Spirit. She had prayed for the baptism, but had not yet received it. As I was leaving her apartment one day, she stopped me and told me about a dream she had. She said she dreamt that she was being immersed in a big tub of holy water. When she came out of the holy water, she saw letters in front of her that spelled out JESUS! I laughed to myself when I heard this because the woman really did not know what the dream meant! She didn't have the understanding that baptism was to be done by full immersion rather than sprinkling.

I was teaching Bible studies on the topic of forgiveness at the coffeehouse one summer. One of the women stopped me dead in my tracks and demanded to know how I came up with that topic. Apparently, God had been dealing with her on forgiveness. I simply told her God had led me to teach on that particular subject that night.

What is the difference between revival and evangelism? Revival is for the church, reviving something that had once been alive. Evangelism is bringing life to those who never have been saved. Christians receive life from Christ when they become born again, but if they become lukewarm, they need revival. The place for revival is inside the church building. The place for evangelism is outside the church. Let's pray for revival that our churches may be strong and vibrant again. Let's pray for a burden to witness to unsaved people that we may be soul winners!

Chapter 15: Are You Doing Your Father's Business?

Jesus is the Son of God. He is God made manifest in the flesh for the salvation of the world. In the Gospels, Jesus made it clear that He came to do the will of the Father. Jesus went about doing His Father's business. When Jesus was a boy, He went to Jerusalem with His parents at the time of Passover. When they started back home to Nazareth, Joseph and Mary noticed that Jesus was not with them. They found Him in the temple in Jerusalem, talking with the religious leaders. When Mary asked Jesus why He was in the temple, He responded, "Did you not know I would be doing my Father's business?" (Luke 2:48-49).

Every job has a description. The job of a doctor is to treat patients. The job of a teacher is to teach students. The job of a policeman is to enforce the law. The job of a cashier is to ring up a sale. The job of a waitress is to wait on tables. The job of a pilot is to fly airplanes. The job of a mailman is to deliver the mail.

Jesus read His job description out of a scroll on the Sabbath. Luke 4:16-19 says,

And he came to Nazareth, where he had been brought up: and, as his custom was, he went into the synagogue on the sabbath day, and stood up for to read. And there was delivered unto him the book of the prophet Esaias. And when he had

opened the book, he found the place where it was written, the Spirit of the Lord is upon me, because he hath anointed me to preach the gospel to the poor; he hath sent me to heal the brokenhearted, to preach deliverance to the captives, and recovering of sight to the blind, to set at liberty them that are bruised, to preach the acceptable year of the Lord.

What is Jesus' job description? What did He come to do? You may say that He came to die for our sins so that we could have eternal life. Jesus said He came to preach the gospel to the poor, to heal the brokenhearted, and to preach deliverance to the captives.

Jesus had a supernatural healing and miracle ministry. Anywhere He was, He healed the sick and performed miracles. Many people believed in Him because of the works that He did. Crowds followed Him everywhere He went. Jesus' disciples followed Him. Jesus gave His disciples the power and authority to do His work.

The disciples of Jesus had supernatural power just like Jesus had, but they are not the only ones who have power to do mighty works. Miracles did not just happen in the Bible. Jesus is still alive and well today. After Jesus was resurrected from the dead, He instructed His believers to spread the gospel. Mark 16:15-18 says,

And he said unto them, Go ye into all the world, and preach the gospel to every creature. He that believeth and is baptized shall be saved; but he that believeth not shall be damned. And these signs shall follow them that believe; In my name shall they cast out devils; they shall speak with new tongues; they shall take up serpents; and if they

*drink any deadly thing, it shall not hurt them; they
shall lay hands on the sick, and they shall recover.*

Jesus told us that these signs would follow those who believe.
This is called the Great Commission and is the job description
of every believer in Jesus. So what is our job description? What
is our Father's business? Many times a father wants to pass
his business down to his son so it will continue. Our heavenly
Father wants us to go about doing His business. His business is
to heal the sick, raise the dead, cleanse the lepers, and cast out
devils. It is to cause the blind to see, the deaf to hear, and the
lame to walk (Matthew 10:7-8).

Do you believe in miracles? Do you believe that Jesus can
heal the sick today? Do you believe that the church has power
to do mighty works? Where does this power come from? Jesus
told His believers to wait for the promise of the Holy Ghost.
Before He ascended into heaven, Jesus told the disciples to
wait in Jerusalem until they were filled with power from on
high. When we are filled with the Holy Spirit, we receive the
potential to operate in the power of God. Jesus gave us the
authority to do the works of His ministry.

Do you desire power to do the works that Jesus did? Do
you believe that God can use you to do mighty works? Have
you surrendered your life to Jesus Christ? If not, pray and
repent and allow Him to rescue you. If so, He wants to fill you
with the power of the Holy Ghost! If you would like to receive
this power, pray to be filled with Holy Ghost power!

Chapter 16: America, Do Not Forget Your God

What is the role of religion in American life? Is it true that our founding fathers intended our nation to be strictly secular? Or was it their goal to set up a Christian commonwealth? Our founding fathers intended a Christian nation and a secular government; this is known as the separation of church and state. The Constitution establishes America as a Christian nation. America was established upon Christian beliefs, and today remains the most Christian nation in the world.

When we are saved and become Christians, God brings us out of a life of sin. Jesus Christ died so that we may have salvation and healing. God delivers us in the same way that He led Israel out of slavery in Egypt. After God brought His people out of bondage, they began a journey toward the Promised Land. The Promised Land was Israel's inheritance.

God brought the Israelites out of slavery in Egypt by doing great miracles. God divided the Red Sea so Israel could cross over; then He closed it and caused Pharaoh and his army to drown. After they left Egypt, Israel entered the wilderness. God promised the people they would defeat their enemies and enter the Promised Land. Moses told the people that it was a land of plenty, flowing with milk and honey. God's covenant blessings brought Israel great prosperity. Joshua and the people of Israel had great success when they entered the

Promised Land. They defeated their enemies and possessed the land.

Moses warned the people not to forget the Lord their God after they were settled, satisfied, and prosperous in the Promised Land. This warning can be found in Deuteronomy 8:11-19.

Just as God gave promises to the nation of Israel, He gives Christians promises and a destiny. When we become born again, we are given purpose and a calling. God has a plan that He wants to fulfill in your life.

Americans are upset because of what we see happening in our nation today. This last decade has been difficult and people are wondering if God has forsaken America. Where was God on 9/11? The answer to this question is obvious. God was right where America had put Him—out of the nation. America has pushed God out by taking prayer out of the schools and the Ten Commandments out of the courts. When the Israelites rejected their God and began to serve false gods and idols, their enemies defeated them. Moses warned Israel to remember the Lord their God, or else they would be destroyed. America was founded as a Christian nation; we served the Lord our God until we became prosperous and satisfied.

Many of the first colonists came to New England for the freedom to practice their faith. The Pilgrims founded Plymouth Colony; they had separated from the Church of England and were called Separatists. Other colonists distrusted the Church of England, and the king authorized the establishment of new religious settlements in America. The Puritans wanted to establish a Christian society and settled in Massachusetts primarily. Roger Williams established Rhode Island to be able to worship God. All of the New England colonies were settled as Christian communities. Other colonies were established for the same reason—religious freedom. Pennsylvania began as a Quaker community and allowed everyone to worship as they pleased. Because of America's Christian roots and heritage, God blessed and prospered our nation greatly.

America has been the wealthiest, greatest country in the world. Whenever a nation commits itself to serve God, God will bring blessings. The national religion of Haiti was voodoo and witchcraft; Haiti is one of the world's poorest nations. When the 2010 earthquake devastated that country, Haitians literally were brought to their knees. However, something great has happened since the Haiti earthquake. Their president has repented and renounced voodoo, declaring Christianity the religion of Haiti. This has caused great revival, and many Haitians have been saved.

In 2006, Barack Obama gave a speech that shook many believers. Our President has actually declared that America is no longer a Christian nation!

After Israel possessed the Promised Land and lived in peace, Joshua gave them a warning. Joshua 24:14-15 says,

> *Now therefore fear the Lord, and serve him in sincerity and in truth: and put away the gods which your fathers served on the other side of the flood, and in Egypt; and serve ye the Lord. And if it seem evil unto you to serve the Lord, choose you this day whom ye will serve; whether the gods which your fathers served that were on the other side of the flood, or the gods of the Amorites, in whose land ye dwell: but as for me and my house, we will serve the Lord.*

Come, Holy Spirit

Verses 20-22 say,

*If ye forsake the Lord, and serve strange gods, then
he will turn and do you hurt, and consume you, after
that he hath done you good. And the people said
unto Joshua, Nay; but we will serve the Lord. And
Joshua said unto the people, Ye are witnesses against
yourselves that ye have chosen you the Lord, to serve
him. And they said, We are witnesses.*

The Moravian Christian community also eventually
settled in America—first in Georgia and later Pennsylvania—
to escape European persecution. In 1727, the Moravians
gathered together in their home community in Germany to
pray and seek God. The entire church felt the presence of the
Holy Spirit and began to repent of their sins—even those out
in the field and not at the meeting. They were transformed and
renewed. Shortly after this powerful service, the Moravians
began the practice of hourly prayer. In this prayer chain,
people would take turns praying every hour of the day. They
continued this prayer chain for one hundred years. After
America won the Revolutionary War, the government sent a
proclamation throughout the colonies asking them to observe
a day of prayer. The Moravians in North Carolina observe
every Fourth of July with a worship and prayer service.

Just as God blessed Israel after they settled the Promised
Land, God has blessed this nation. America is a Christian
nation that has prospered above all others in wealth and
military strength. But America has forgotten her God.
America has opened her doors to immorality, materialism,
entertainment, pornography, idolatry, witchcraft, abortion,
homosexuality, false religions, and many other sins.

After Joshua was gone, Israel turned away from God and began to serve false gods. They were defeated by their enemies.

In 2006, the real estate market declined and houses went into foreclosure. Then the stock market collapsed. Since 2008, America has been in a recession. Many times, what happens in the natural world is a reflection of something happening in the spiritual world. When there is a shaking in the natural, it can cause a spiritual awakening. America has forgotten and turned away from God, and it is time for our nation to repent so that God may restore us and bring healing to our land.

If there ever was a time to call upon God, it is now. In America, we cannot afford to repeat the mistakes of Old Testament Israel by forgetting our God. When disaster strikes a nation, the hearts of many are turned toward God, and the hearts of others are turned away. Many people fail to see the sin of this nation or the way people have forgotten God and turned aside to serve other gods.

Throughout history, there has been darkness as well as revival. Revivals begin in the hearts of God's people during periods of moral darkness and national depression. There must be an increase in prayer, fasting, and repentance, as well as a burden to see souls saved. There is a shaking taking place in America because of the recession. Revival is coming to this nation, and people will turn to the Lord. This will bring about a change in this country. The end result will be a mighty move of God and many souls will be saved. Are you ready for this revival?

President Obama has declared that America is no longer a Christian nation. If we take God and Christianity out of America, a door is opened for our enemies to attack our nation. Many people feel that America has changed for the worse and they want their country back. It is time for America to repent and turn back to God.

Chapter 17: A Warning to the Church in America

The book of Acts records that some people (religious leaders) didn't like what the disciples were doing in the early church. They didn't like it when the sick were healed and the gospel was preached. They didn't like the miracles, signs, and wonders. If they didn't like it in the Bible times, do you think the enemy likes it today?

The religious leaders rose up against the early church. They told the disciples to be quiet. They told them not to teach, speak, or do anything in Jesus' name. They tried to get the disciples to shut up and sit down. They wanted the disciples to stop preaching the gospel. Eventually some of the disciples got thrown into prison because of the gospel. But even in prison, the disciples did not get discouraged. Instead they actually thanked God that they were counted worthy to suffer for His name's sake. When we think about how the Lord suffered for us, it should be a small thing for us to lay down our own lives for the One who died for us. Is it a horrible thing if we suffer sometimes for the sake of the gospel? In the early church, they counted it all joy. They considered it an honor.

I am concerned about the church in America today. Because of political correctness, it seems like the culture is trying to dictate right from wrong. But the world is not supposed to determine morality: the Word of God does. In the

Bible it says that in the last days, there will be a falling away, a decline in morality. In 2 Timothy 3:1-5 it says,

> *This know also, that in the last days perilous times shall come. For men shall be lovers of their own selves, covetous, boasters, proud, blasphemers, disobedient to parents, unthankful, unholy, without natural affection, trucebreakers, false accusers, incontinent, fierce, despisers of those that are good, traitors, heady, highminded, lovers of pleasures more than lovers of God; having a form of godliness, but denying the power thereof: from such turn away.*

The Bible says that man will be doing what is right in his own eyes, calling evil good and good evil. I want to caution the church in America. I want to give a warning. The church needs to understand that if the world is trying to tell you what to say and believe, you better not listen. The church is not supposed to conform to the world—the world should conform to the church.

The church is supposed to be the standard, based on the Word of God. We have to hold up the standard of the Bible. This is not our opinion, this is the Word of God. The world is not supposed to determine morality or the church's teaching. The only standard we have in the church is the Bible.

If someone tells you to preach something different than what the Bible says, you refuse. You teach and preach what the Word of God says. I want to caution the American church and give you a word. If you want to stand for something other than what the Word of God says, you fear man more than you fear God. That is a wrong position. You don't want to have fear of man.

Melinda Bauman

Do not fear man, pastors in America. Yes, the gospel is offensive. We cut down the spirit of compromise in the name of Jesus. Pastors, don't you know that you are not supposed to preach what people want to hear? You are not supposed to tickle ears. In 2 Timothy 4:2-4 it says,

> *Preach the word; be instant in season, out of season; reprove, rebuke, exhort with all longsuffering and doctrine. For the time will come when they will not endure sound doctrine; but after their own lusts shall they heap to themselves teachers, having itching ears; and they shall turn away their ears from the truth, and shall be turned unto fables.*

Do you think that telling people what they want to hear will cause you to have a large church and a lot of money come into the offering plate? We are preachers, not politicians. Politicians pander by appealing to different voting groups, telling voters what they want to hear in order to get votes. This is why politicians say conflicting things, depending on what group they are addressing.

Politicians are trying to get elected, so they do whatever the people want. They allow themselves to be controlled by people. If you are a minister and a preacher, you don't have to do what people tell you to do. Our boss is not the people; our boss is Jesus Christ. We say the words He wants us to say and do what He wants us to do. If that offends people, that is no surprise. We know that many people are offended by the gospel. They don't want to hear words of sound doctrine; they have itching ears.

People don't want to hear anything that's going to challenge them. They just want to hear a feel-good message and a seeker-friendly gospel. They don't want to be confronted

101

about their sins. They don't want repentance. They want to live and do what they want. They come to church if they feel like it. There is no commitment or sacrifice; there's no dedication to the church, just consumerism.

An entertainment mentality has come into the church. People come to church as spectators to see the show. If people like the show, then they leave a good offering. If they don't like what they hear, then they go somewhere else. They go find a church where they can be entertained and told what they want to hear—a seeker-friendly church. If that's the way the church has become in America, we need some desperate prayer.

The American church needs pastors who do not compromise the message of the gospel. We need preachers who will honor God and obey His Word. We need preachers who will say it like it is and not worry about pleasing man. As ministers of the gospel, we only should be concerned about pleasing God. We are preachers, not pandering politicians. We are called by God, not by man. It is not our job to be seeker-sensitive—we are to be God-sensitive. We are not to be politically correct; we are not running for political office.

Church in America, we should only be seeking to please and serve Jesus Christ. The gospel is a non-compromising message and people will take it or leave it. We don't change the message of the gospel. We are simply the messengers. We deliver the message to the people and leave it to the Holy Spirit to gather the harvest of souls.

We need to be like the apostles in the early church described in Acts who feared God more than man. Some people will be offended and reject the gospel, but some will accept. If people reject the message of salvation, then they are rejecting God, not you. Do not take it personally when people say you are prejudiced for taking a stand against sin.

I have said goodbye and watched people leave our church because they were not interested in the uncompromised, full gospel of Jesus Christ. Unfortunately, they did not have to travel far to find a dead church that preached a watered-down gospel and let them live whatever lifestyle they wanted—as long as they attended service on Sunday and left an offering.

People might attack you for saying that abortion is murder and homosexuality is sin. People may judge you for saying that Christianity is the only way to heaven. People may hate you for saying there is only one way to heaven—through our Lord and Savior Jesus Christ. There are not many paths to God. There is only one way, and His name is Jesus Christ. All other gods and religions will lead a person to spiritual death and condemnation in hell. We love people and want to see them saved; we preach the full truth of the gospel. We want to win souls so that they may be with us in heaven for eternity. We have no right to pick and choose which part of the Bible is valid; the whole Word of God is truth. Heaven and earth may pass away, but God's Word will never perish or fail.

I pray for the church and for preachers to stand for truth, even if it means that people get offended and leave the church. People need to be convicted by the Word and get right with God rather than continue to live in sin. Lord God, give the church a backbone. Give the pastors boldness to not compromise the Word of God or be controlled by money or Jezebel.

Why do you think so many churches today have fallen away from preaching about speaking in tongues and the power of the Holy Spirit? Our enemy, the devil, hates the Holy Spirit, and he has caused people to be offended by tongues.

103

Come, Holy Spirit

Even Pentecostal or charismatic churches, which claim to be Spirit-filled and believe in the baptism of the Holy Spirit, have turned away.

What is going on in the Spirit-filled churches today that don't preach about the Holy Spirit? The people are not operating in the power of the Holy Spirit or practicing the spiritual gifts. The Spirit is not moving in their church services, and there are no altar calls or prayer times to be filled the baptism of the Holy Spirit. I pray for the church in America that we might not grieve the Spirit of God.

Some people might come into your church—seeker-friendly people who want to hear a feel-good gospel. These people want their ears tickled; they do not want to hear a sermon about sin and repentance. They are not interested in the baptism of the Holy Spirit evidenced by speaking in tongues. They may even try to control you by telling you what to preach. This is a control spirit. Pastors, you need to be aware of two controlling spirits in the church—Jezebel and Absalom.

The controlling spirit of Jezebel wants to control the pastor, and the spirit of Absalom wants to lead a rebellion and split the church. The Jezebel spirit will tell you what to preach. People may tell you that speaking in tongues is not for them and not to preach about it. When people try to control what you preach, you better not listen. You need to preach what God is saying, not what people want to hear. Preachers, you need to fear God more than man. Don't start listening to people and controlling spirits. If they leave the church, you didn't want them there anyway. Controlling spirits, especially Jezebel and Absalom, want to destroy the church. Church splits are painful and cause much hurt to God's people. Some may get so wounded that they never trust a church family again.

Melinda Bauman

People may be offended at the truth of the full gospel and leave your church. They don't want to hear sound doctrine and the uncompromised Word of God. I advise pastors to preach what God tells them to preach. It might not be a pretty sermon. You may need to tell your people to repent for the kingdom of heaven is at hand and Jesus is coming soon. People need to lay down their sinful lifestyles and get right with God.

Church in America, we are the standard. We are standing for the truth of the Word of God. We do not allow the enemy to infiltrate and take over the church. We do not allow the ways of the world to change the church. The world is to conform to the church; the church is not to conform to the world. Modern culture and society do not tell the church what to preach and believe. We want sinners to come into church, but we expect them to change. You come as you are, but you don't stay that way. You come into the church as a lost sinner, but you find salvation, healing, and deliverance when you get here.

A saved person is changed—old things are passed away. Being born again means you have a brand new life. Thank You, God, for the power of the gospel and the blood of Jesus which change lives. Thank You for power to heal the sick and brokenhearted and to set the captives free. Thank You for Holy Ghost power! The blood of Jesus will never lose its power to save and change a person—power to heal a broken life, break the bondage of sin, and heal diseases. The anointing of God destroys the yokes of spiritual bondage. The anointing is the presence of God. Isaiah 10:27 says, "And it shall come to pass in that day, that his burden shall be taken away from off thy shoulder, and his yoke from off thy neck, and the yoke shall be destroyed because of the anointing."

God, I pray that the church would not only operate in the spiritual gifts, but also in the fruit of the Spirit. Help the ministers to have the Christian character and lifestyle to back up the anointing that flows through them. Raise the standard in the church that we would both operate in Your power and walk in Your holiness. I pray You would raise up ministers who have integrity, who are not struggling with sin in their own lives.

I pray that confidence would be restored to the church and its ministry. Develop character and integrity in the ministers of the gospel. Teach them humility and keep them from spiritual pride. Restore respect and integrity to the office of the pulpit. Heal those people who have been hurt and spiritually abused by controlling pastors. Bring healing and restoration to Your church, Lord God. Remove the false shepherds and wolves in sheep's clothing who devour the flock. Raise up good shepherds—those who will love and care for the sheep.

I pray that ministers would walk in a high standard of character. Heal the hurts caused by evangelists and pastors falling into sin, misusing church money, and letting people down. Bring healing to those who were betrayed by their church leaders. Restore the fear of the Lord to the office of the pulpit. The ministers must have a life that is upright before God and the people. Restore trust and honor to the office of the ministry. Judgment begins in the house of God.

God, restore the church and put her in order. We are the bride of Christ. We must have our garments pure, clean, white, and ready for the Bridegroom's soon coming. Jesus, take away any spot or blemish from Your bride, the church. Help us to be pure and holy vessels. Cleanse, purify, and wash us in Your blood, Lord Jesus.

Chapter 18: Keepers of the Flame, a Prophetic Word

And Nadab and Abihu, the sons of Aaron, took either of them his censer, and put fire therein, and put incense thereon, and offered strange fire before the Lord, which he commanded them not. And there went out fire from the Lord, and devoured them, and they died before the Lord. Then Moses said unto Aaron, This is it that the Lord spake, saying, I will be sanctified in them that come nigh me, and before all the people I will be glorified. And Aaron held his peace (Leviticus 10:1-3).

I hear the Lord say, "Keepers of the flame." The Lord says that He is looking for keepers of the flame. He is looking for those who can tend to the fire of God. Looking for those who will be faithful to serve upon the altar and faithfully minister to the fire of God—for those who will be keepers of the flame. The Lord says, "Not everyone can be trusted to keep the fire burning on the altar." The Lord says that there are those who are keepers of false fire, or strange fire, because they have corrupted the altar of God.

When the priesthood was set up in the Old Testament, priests were sanctified and ordained into the priesthood. Their job was to minister to the fire of God that burned upon the altar.

This represents the presence of God where the glory of God dwelt in the ark of the covenant. There was a golden candlestick and a fire burning upon the altar of sacrifice in the temple.

The Lord says, "There were those in the priesthood who did not offer pure fire. They offered up strange fire that was displeasing to Me. I had to destroy those who offered up strange fire. The strange fire occurred because the priests had corrupted the flame. They were not good keepers of the fire of God."

There is fire that comes from God. The Holy Spirit comes as fire. God wants to send His fire like the fire that fell down and consumed Elijah's altar when he prayed. God wants to send holy fire, not strange fire. The Lord must have people who are keepers of the fire, who are faithful, who will not corrupt the fire and turn it into a profane thing.

The Lord says that He is searching for keepers of the flame—for faithful, pure workers. He is searching for ministers who will be faithful to attend to the fire of God, who will keep the flame of God. They will not pervert or corrupt the fire because of their own wickedness. There were people in the Old Testament, priests who were not faithful to keep the flame of God. They offered up strange fire. They were corrupt and full of sin, and God had to remove them.

The same thing applies today. There are some ministers who are not full of integrity. They are not living a pure life, and they have caused profane things in the house of God. They have caused strange fire to burn. But the Lord says, "I want to release My fire. I want to release pure fire, the true flame of God."

The Lord says, "I am looking for keepers of the flame. For those who are pure and walking uprightly before Me." The Lord says, "I cannot release my glory and fire and keep it burning unless there are keepers of the flame—people who will not profane and turn the fire of God into strange fire."

The Lord says, "I want to release my fire, but I have to find those who are faithful keepers of the flame—those who will not use it for their own glory or take credit for it. I cannot work through those people who will turn it into a profane thing." The Lord wants to release His fire in a powerful way, but He must find those who will be faithful keepers of the flame.

Lord, I pray that true servants of God will rise up, those without agendas and motives, those who are not self-seeking and living in sin. Lord, I ask that You raise up integrity in Your keepers of the flame; I pray that you raise up people who know how to receive and steward the fire in their churches. Raise up stewards who will keep the fire of God burning. We know that You want to send revival fire, but it must be sustained. So many times revival is not sustained because the ministers do not know how to keep the fire burning. They fall into sin or use revival for their own selfish interests. Raise up good stewards who will not turn it into strange fire and then have to be removed. The Lord will not share His glory with another.

Raise up those who are not trying to make a name for themselves, who are not self-seeking. Raise up faithful ministers who serve You because they love You and not for any selfish motives. You want to send revival in a mighty way, but the fire must be released in a place where it can be sustained, or it will go out.

You, oh God, will not burn in a place where the people will not sustain the fire. You must find people who are good keepers of the flame so that Your glory can be released. We pray that Your fire will continue to burn, and not go out because of man's sinful ways. We thank You, Lord, for releasing Your glory. Help us to be faithful to steward the fire of God. I release this word now in Jesus' name. Amen.

About Melinda Bauman

Melinda Bauman was filled with the Holy Spirit in a Pentecostal church in 1990 and felt the call of God on her life.

In 2003, she began holding weekly Bible studies out of a coffeehouse in Euclid, Ohio, and later in Wickliffe. She obtained a Pentecostal minister's license in 2005 and began holding monthly revival church services. The services demonstrated the spiritual gifts and power of God to the church. Different speakers ministered at these services in the areas of prophecy, healing, and deliverance.

Melinda began to pray about obtaining a property and starting a church. God provided a building in Eastlake, Ohio, and Worldwide Great Commission Fellowship's first church service was held in April 2007.

The goal of the church is to fulfill the Great Commission (Mark 16:15) by spreading the gospel message of salvation, healing, and deliverance through our Lord and Savior, Jesus Christ.

www.worldwidegcf.com

More Titles by 5 Fold Media

Release from Invisible Barriers
by Terry Smith
$12.95
ISBN: 978-1-936578-32-0

Release from Invisible Barriers is an interactive workbook that is designed to be a personal "workshop" between you and the Lord; through cooperation with the Holy Spirit, it will lead you to find and remove "invisible barriers."

A very versatile tool, this workbook can be used in two different ways. You can systemically read, pray, and apply your way through this workbook from cover to cover, as each chapter builds upon the one before it. Or, it can be used as a reference and ministry manual with each chapter standing alone.

Who Needs God?
by George Downes
$11.95
ISBN: 978-1-936578-34-4

When we look at where our society is today, it is not hard to see the lack of godly truth and spiritual values. We have to admit that God is not even considered as a point of purpose in the affairs of humanity, never mind creation. As a society, we have lost all concern for absolute moral values. The frightening realization is that a "who cares" attitude is also creeping into the church.

Who Needs God? will open up the thinking of our generation to the truth of God's identity, and will address our responsibility to teach and train our youth in the knowledge of His truth.

Like 5 Fold Media on Facebook, follow us on Twitter!

5 Fold Media, LLC is a Christ-centered media company. Our desire is to produce lasting fruit in writing, music, art, and creative gifts.

"To Establish and Reveal"
For more information visit:
www.5foldmedia.com

Use your mobile device to scan the tag above and visit our website.
Get the free app: http://gettag. mobi

CPSIA information can be obtained at www.ICGtesting.com
Printed in the USA
BVOW04s0634100614

355941BV00002B/11/P

9 781936 578450